AVE MARIA!

For more copies of this booklet and other Marian titles visit:

AcademyoftheImmaculate.com

IMPRIMI POTEST

Fr. Immacolato M. Acquali, FI

Minister General, Franciscan Friars of the Immaculate

December 8, 2022

*Solemnity of the Immaculate Conception
of the Blessed Virgin Mary*

IMPRIMATUR

Most Reverend Edgard M. da Cunha, SDV

Bishop of Fall River, Massachusetts

February 2, 2023

Feast of the Presentation of Our Lord in the Temple

(The nihil obstat and imprimatur are official declarations that a book or pamphlet is free from doctrinal or moral error. No implication is contained therein that those who grant the nihil obstat or imprimatur agree with the contents or statements expressed.)

PREPARATION FOR
TOTAL CONSECRATION
TO THE IMMACULATE
ACCORDING TO SAINT MAXIMILIAN M. KOLBE

Fr. Matthias M. Sasko, FI

TABLE OF CONTENTS

FIRST FIVE DAYS
UNLESS YOU BECOME LIKE A LITTLE CHILD

WEEK 1
COME TO THE THRONE OF GRACE

WEEK 2
TAKE HER INTO YOUR HOME

WEEK 3
BECOME LIKE YOUR MOTHER

WEEK 4
LET YOURSELF BE GUIDED BY HER

Who are You, O Immaculate?

Immaculate, Queen of Heaven and earth, I know that I am unworthy to approach You—to fall on my knees before You with my forehead to the ground. But because I know of Your goodness and love for me, and because I wish to love You in return, I beg You to be so good as to allow me to come to You, and I beseech You to tell me who You are, so that I may know You and love You ever more. I desire to know You ever better, without limits, and to love You ever more fervently without any reserve.

You are *the Immaculate Conception*, *the Immaculate One*, and this is truly Your name, a name by which You love to be called. It is a name unique to You and You alone. You are not God or an Angel, neither of whom are conceived. You are indeed a real human conception—conceived by Your holy parents, Joachim and Anne. But neither are You any mere daughter of Adam, because though they are all conceived, they nevertheless cannot be called immaculate. You and You alone are *the Immaculate Conception*, *the Immaculate One*.

Human words do not suffice to speak of You—because even the loftiest ones are never free from imperfection—whereas You are simply immaculate, without any stain or imperfection, all beautiful and full of grace. Our human knowledge about You is therefore still so deficient. You alone must reveal Yourself to our souls that we may know You as You really are.

We call You Lady, but this is not enough to express who You are for us. We call You Queen, as indeed You are, but this also is too little. We dare to call You our Mother, but not even this suffices. We call You all these things, and You are all of them—but none of them, not even taken all together, express what God has made You, and Who You are for us.

I wish to know You, O Immaculate, because I wish to love You and thank You for all that You are. I wish to give myself to You totally and entirely—with my soul, my body, my all—so as to express my thankfulness to You for what You are for me.

With longing therefore I await the day when all things are made known, when our good Lord will show me all that You have been for me in life, how many unknown graces You have obtained for me to form me into Christ, Your first-born Son. I wish to be Yours, to belong to You both on earth and in Heaven, and to praise You, and together with You, to praise and love God for all eternity. Amen.

How to use this booklet

This booklet is written as a day-by-day guide to arrive at a very specific goal: your total consecration to the Immaculate. Why do you need a daily guide to reach this goal? You know that at every period of its history, our world moves at a certain pace. In our times, it is a fast pace—so fast a pace that, in keeping up with it, you might be struggling to not forget your soul, its salvation, and its sanctification. Hopefully, this little day-by-day guide will motivate you and help you to find time every day for your soul, even in the midst of the busyness of a fast-paced life like yours.

The obvious way to use this booklet is to follow it day by day. If you wish to arrive at the goal of your total consecration to the Immaculate, you should make a diligent effort not to miss a single day. If you do miss a day, however, there is no need to start all over. You can make up the missed day and just keep going.[1]

Once you have consecrated yourself to Her, you might still find the booklet useful in preparing to renew your consecration every year, or as a daily meditation booklet to help you live your consecration faithfully and fervently. As you read and reread, always remember: Our Lady has drawn you to this little booklet because She wants you for Herself. Jesus gave you to Her, and Her to you. She wants you to recognize this priceless gift and to live your life by it. If you only let Her, Our Lady will indeed take you completely to Herself, as Her possession and property. You will belong to Her, and through Her to Jesus in the surest, safest and most beautiful way.

---

[1] Missing a day will throw off your consecration date. To remedy this, you can certainly try to do two days' meditations in one day to catch up. If for some reason this does not work, however, and you cannot make your original consecration date, do not give up! You can make your consecration on whatever day you end, or on the Saturday closest, because every Saturday is particularly dedicated to Our Lady. You don't have to wait until the next Marian feast, especially if it is far off. Our Lady wants You for Herself without delay.

CHOOSE A DATE

No lengthy preparation is absolutely necessary for consecration to Our Lady. It can be done in an instant, with just one act of your will. If you want to belong to Her, make sure to tell Her right away, and you will indeed already be Hers.

A time of preparation for consecration is nevertheless very desirable—especially because it will allow you to realize who the Immaculate is and what it means to give yourself to Her *totally*, and to leave nothing out of your consecration, either by ignorance or negligence.

Choosing a Marian date for your consecration is therefore very helpful. Below is a list of different Marian liturgical feasts and recurrences that you can choose from. On each of these days, the Immaculate gives special graces to those who honor Her.

START DATE	NAME OF FEAST	CONSECRATION DATE
November 29	Mother of God	January 1
December 21	Espousal with St. Joseph	January 23
December 31	Presentation of Our Lord by Our Lady	February 2
January 9	Our Lady of Lourdes	February 11
February 20 (21 if a leap year)	The Annunciation	March 25
Monday of the first week of Lent	Commemoration of Our Lady's Compassion	Friday before Good Friday
Monday of the second week of Lent	Commemoration of Our Lady's faith in the Resurrection	Holy Saturday
March 24	Our Lady of Good Counsel	April 26

START DATE	NAME OF FEAST	CONSECRATION DATE
April 5	Mediatrix of All Graces	May 8
April 10	Our Lady of Fatima	May 13
April 28	The Visitation	May 31
Subtract 33 days and start on that day	May is the month of Mary	Any other day in May
2 weeks before Pentecost	Immaculate Heart of Mary	Saturday after the Solemnity of the Most Sacred Heart of Jesus
May 25	Our Lady of Perpetual Help	June 27
June 13	Our Lady of Mt. Carmel	July 16
June 30	Queen of Angels	August 2
July 13	The Assumption	August 15
July 20	Queenship of Mary	August 22
July 24	Seven Joys of Our Lady	August 26
August 6	The Birth of Our Lady	September 8
August 13	Our Lady of Sorrows	September 15
August 22	Our Lady of Ransom	September 24
September 4	Our Lady of the Rosary	October 7
October 19	Presentation of Our Lady in the Temple	November 21
November 5	The Immaculate Conception	December 8
November 9	Our Lady of Guadalupe	December 12
November 13	Queen of the Franciscan Order	December 15
Subtract 33 days and start on that day	Every Saturday is dedicated to Our Lady	Any Saturday of the year

THE SOURCES AND SPIRIT
of This Booklet

Saint Maximilian M. Kolbe, who—in the words of St. Paul VI —can be counted "among the great saints and seers who have understood, venerated and sung the mystery of Mary" (*Beatification Homily*, October 17, 1971), is the primary source of this short booklet. Born in 1894 in Poland, he became a Franciscan friar at 16 years old and in 1917 founded the Militia of the Immaculate. He dedicated his whole Franciscan life to the cause of his religious order, which is the cause of the Immaculate: making Our Lady known and loved, so as to conquer the whole world to Christ through Her. He was the founder of the world's largest friary, Niepokalanów ("The City of the Immaculate") in Poland, which at its peak counted over 800 souls consecrated to Our Lady and to Her work. He was also a pioneer of evangelization through mass media, achieving the largest Catholic periodical both in Poland as well as in Japan, where he founded a mission. Perfectly conformed to the Redeemer by His Lady and Queen, he died on August 14, 1941, voluntarily sacrificing his life to die of starvation to save a fellow prisoner at Auschwitz concentration camp.

This booklet was written as much as possible in the words and spirit of St. Maximilian M. Kolbe himself, as well as of other saints and holy persons who wrote about Our Lady and whose spirituality the saint recognized as his own. It is not original, nor is it meant to be original.

Because this is not a scholarly book, and to avoid making the text cumbersome and unreadable, the sources are intentionally omitted, except for the most important teachings of the Church.

FIRST FIVE DAYS

Unless You Become Like a Little Child

DAY 1 — SPIRITUAL CHILDHOOD

> *At that time the disciples came to Jesus saying,*
> *"Who is the greatest in the kingdom of heaven?*
> *And calling to him a child, he put him in the midst of them,*
> *and said, "Truly I say to you, unless you turn and become*
> *like children, you will never enter the kingdom of heaven.*
> *Whoever humbles himself like this little child,*
> *he is the greatest in the kingdom of heaven."*
>
> — MATTHEW 18:1–4

hen Our Lord spoke these holy words, He thought of you. He had in His mind a specific Father for you, His own Father, the One Who is in Heaven. He also had in His Mind a specific Mother for you, His very own Mother, Mary. He proclaimed Her to you publicly from the cross, before He died, saying: "Behold your Mother" (Jn 19:27). But He made you Her child even since the Annunciation and the Incarnation.

Jesus and you are members of the same family: He is your brother, because you both have the same Father and Mother. Jesus—the Son of God and the Son of Mary—wants you to become perfectly like Him: a child of God and a child of Mary. If you take careful note that Our Lord loves to call Himself the "Son of man" in the holy Gospels, you will understand that it is because He loves to remind you of His virginal conception and birth from Mary. Rejoice in this grace, which He has deigned to share with you.

The Church teaches us that ever since the Second Person of the Holy Trinity became man and our brother in the womb of Mary, any relationship with Him and His Father will imply a Mother-son relationship with Mary as well (cf. St. John Paul II, *Homily*, 30 November 1979). If, therefore, you wish to be a true child of God and an heir of the Kingdom of your heavenly Father, you must love your spiritual Mother, and you must love Her as Jesus loves Her.

Think what a special gift Our Lord wants to bestow upon you: "Whoever humbles himself like this little child, he is the greatest in the kingdom of heaven" (Mt 18:1–4). He wants to give you the grace of perfect spiritual childhood, and, therefore also the greatest and most special place in His Kingdom, close to His heavenly Mother and yours. What joy must fill your heart at this amazing thought of the goodness of Jesus towards you!

Daily Prayers (pp. 77–78)

DAY 2 — A PEARL OF GREAT PRICE

Flesh and blood has not revealed this to you,
but my Father who is in Heaven.

— MATTHEW 16:17

he attraction that you feel to consecrate yourself to the Immaculate is a purely supernatural gift, a grace from above, from the depths of the Heart of God Himself. It was a burning desire that Our Lord carried in His Heart during His whole life, and especially during His Passion. He did not consider His work of Redemption finished until He entrusted St. John the beloved disciple to Mary and until the disciple took Her into his home. St. John, on his part, represented the whole Church—and therefore you as well—which Jesus was entrusting to Our Lady.

It is a pure grace which you did not merit—which no one can merit—but which God, nevertheless, wants to bestow upon you in His great goodness. It is a mystery of love, a pearl of great price, for which it is worth selling everything. Although you will neither understand nor fully appreciate its value until God Himself reveals its value to you on the last day, when all things are made known, you must do all in your power to possess it.

Consecration to Our Lady—you must remember this!—is a grace which, like all grace, not everyone accepts, not even when offered. Remember that, like anyone else, you too can be unfaithful and resist it. You can lose it, and deserve the words of lament that Our Lord pronounced for so many poor souls who do indeed reject and lose this pearl: "O Jerusalem… How often would I have gathered your children together as a hen gathers her brood under her wings, and you would not! Behold your house is forsaken and desolate" (Mt 23:37). Oh, if you only understood how ardent the desire of the Sacred Heart of Jesus is to see you safe under the mantle of Our Lady—like chicks gathered under the wings of a hen—and how sad He is that so many souls refuse, and remain forsaken and desolate, without grace. Pray to Our Lady to not permit you to lose this most precious grace!

Daily Prayers (pp. 77–78)

DAY 3 — A GIFT RECEIVED ON CALVARY

Jesus told his disciples, "If any man would come after me, let him deny himself and take up his cross and follow me."

— MATTHEW 16:24

 ecoming a child of Mary is a gift which Our Lord gives on Calvary. To receive this gift, you must deny yourself, take up your cross, and let Mary lead you there, to the foot of the cross, where you too will hear the words spoken to the disciple: "Behold your Mother" (Jn 19:27).

To be led by Mary and to follow Our Lord, you must deny yourself, which means you must deny that part of you that resists the will of God. You carry within you concupiscence, which comes from sin and leads to sin. Because of this concupiscence, there are within you many sinful inclinations, which hinder you and prevent you from following. You must oppose these inclinations, because they are obstacles that stand in your way to being a faithful disciple.

Do not hesitate to deny yourself. Do not let the sight of your sins and your strong attachment to them discourage you. Our Lady will gently, but powerfully, set you free, and you will be amazed at what She will accomplish in you. Our Lady is the Mother of the Almighty God for whom nothing is impossible, nothing is difficult, who is infinitely greater than your greatest sin!

Make up your mind to fight, so as to overcome your sins. Make a firm decision to confess them and to sin no more. Be vigilant lest you fall—and if you should have the misfortune to fall back into any sin out of weakness and pride, do not for a second doubt Our Lady's love for you and do not wait even for a moment to get up again. Even if satan makes a soul fall very low, his victory is not definitive as long as that soul holds on to its devotion to Her.

Seek therefore to always maintain a pure conscience in Her sight. Make sure to do all that is in your power to be faithful, and trust that Our Lady will do the rest. When you are tempted and feel overwhelmed, have prompt recourse to Her, like a child who turns to its mother in the face of a danger it cannot face on its own. If you do this, She will surely protect you from falling and will make you a faithful follower of Her Son, even unto Calvary itself.

Daily Prayers (pp. 77–78)

DAY 4 – FROM THE HEART OF GOD

*In this is love, not that we have loved God but that he loved us
and sent his Son to be the expiation for our sins…
We love, because he first loved us.*

— 1 John 4:10,19

t is not because of your own goodness that you have
received the grace of being called to total consecration to the Immaculate. It is because of the infinite
goodness of God, whose Heart goes out especially
to those who are most in need of His mercy. It is also because
of the goodness of the Immaculate, who has said "Yes" to God
and lovingly consented to being your Mother. It is She who is
drawing you close to Herself, because She especially loves Her
littlest and weakest children. And such a one are you.

Do not let yourself be deceived by the evil one: do not allow
pride to make you think you are better than others for having
received this gift. Remember always that you are not better than
anyone—you are simply more in need of this mercy, and this is
precisely why you were chosen to receive it. But neither can you
allow fear to make you think you are too unworthy to receive
it. You do not have to be "good enough," nor can you be "too
unworthy" to be called to total consecration to the Immaculate
—all you have to do is desire to belong to Our Lady and let Her
do with you what She pleases. No one is good enough, no one
too depraved to receive this grace.

If the sight of your misery deters you, if failed efforts at being
good discourage you, remember: it is for the weakest children
that a mother's heart is most concerned. It is the weakest ones
who need their Mother most and have a special right to be carried in Her arms, close to Her heart. And remember that you are

one of these privileged children: you have a particular need of Her, and that is why She calls you to consecrate yourself to Her.

Daily Prayers (pp. 77–78)

DAY 5 — YOU CAN DO ALL THINGS IN HIM WHO STRENGTHENS YOU

herever Our Lady enters, She obtains the grace of conversion and sanctification. She will convert you and make you become good, She will make you become holy, if only you give yourself to Her totally and without reserve. She will lead you gently, but powerfully, from sin to grace and then from grace to grace, to the very fullness of grace which God wants to give to you through Her motherly hands.

The reason you have failed in the past, and why you continue to fail now and to fall repeatedly into sin, is that you still trust in yourself too much and not enough in Her. Do you realize this? Your pride is still too strong. You are not yet a humble child who trusts his Mother for everything. You are not yet sufficiently grounded in the truth that on your own you can do nothing. Ask yourself: how can you possibly be holy without grace? And how can you have grace without asking for it? How can you receive it in any other way except through Her hands, if God has decreed to give it in no other way except through Her? And how can you receive all the grace which She wants to give you without living a life of close union with Her? And yet, if you examine yourself closely, do you not find that this is exactly what you still try to do? You try to be holy without a life of constant union with your heavenly Mother. Without Her, the Mediatrix of all graces, you can really do nothing good, nothing holy.

When the Blessed Virgin has made your soul understand that you must remain united to Her by constant prayer, then you shall possess the surest pledge of your future sanctity. Pray and beg for this understanding! With Her you can overcome all obstacles and reach the highest peaks of holiness. You can do all things in Him who strengthens you, through the Immaculate! She will make you Hers, and you cannot belong to Her without becoming like Her, full of grace and without belonging to God as She does. She is like a perfect mold which—if you let yourself be formed by Her—will turn all things to your good and gently but surely transform you into Christ.

Daily Prayers (pp. 77–78)

WEEK 1
Come to the Throne of Grace

DAY 6 – YOU NEED GRACE

 od has created you out of His infinite love for you. The purpose of your short life here on earth is to return, out of your love for Him, to the God who loves you. You are called to live in communion with God by sanctifying grace here on earth, and—if you persevere in the love of God and His holy grace until death—to see Him face to face for all eternity in glory. You can easily see how without grace, therefore, you cannot reach the purpose for which you have been created and for which you exist: you cannot live in communion with God and you cannot reach eternal life.

Sanctifying grace is your participation in the life of God your heavenly Father Himself. It is this grace that makes you a child of God and a "sharer in the Divine Nature" (2Pt 1:4). When you possess this precious gift of grace you are elevated by it to be able to act, speak, and think like a true child of God, holy and immaculate in His sight. Because grace truly makes you a child, then it also makes you an heir, an heir to the Kingdom of your Father in Heaven.

Think of how important grace is: without grace, you cannot call God your Father and the Kingdom of God is closed to you. Without grace, you remain a mere child of sinful Adam, separated from the good God—fallen into sin and constantly plunging from sin to more sin, an enemy of the God who loves you. Without grace you are wounded and broken, confused, blind, alone and walking along the wide and easy road that ends in hell and eternal separation from God.

But think immediately of what you are, or what you can be once you receive or are restored to grace: a true child of God, restored to His beautiful image and likeness, made whole again, healed and walking joyfully on the path towards the place in Heaven which Your Father has prepared for you in His house.

And think above all, of how easy it is to receive this gift, how beautiful to persevere in it. It is this for which your heart longs—a life of holiness, a foretaste of Heaven. Our good God ardently wants to give it to you, and He wants you to have it in the most beautiful and surest way: through Mary, His Mother and yours.

Perhaps, in the past, you have not faithfully guarded the grace given to you. Perhaps you have fallen into mortal sin and lived far from God, maybe even for a long time. Or perhaps you have chosen to live a mediocre life of deliberate venial sin, indifferent to becoming a saint. This is not what God has created you for! Think of your supernatural calling, and renew now your commitment to grace which you received for the first time at your Baptism. Look to Our Lady, and in Her presence renew the promises you made then: renounce again satan, renounce his works, renounce his empty promises. Ask your Immaculate Mother to protect this treasure in your soul and to never permit you to lose it again. Consecration to the Immaculate is the greatest assurance of being faithful to your Baptism, and of persevering in grace until the end!

Daily Prayers (pp. 79–80)

DAY 7 — MARY, THE MEDIATRIX OF ALL GRACE

o participation in grace and Divine Nature is possible without the motherly mediation of the Immaculate. The fullness of grace which God has placed in Her immaculate soul is a source of grace for all the rest of His children. In His infinite wisdom, He does not transmit His Divine life to you except through Her. You therefore cannot have the life of God in your soul unless you also have the life of Mary. You cannot have God for Father unless you have Mary for Mother. God does not give a single grace without Her: "There is no fruit of grace in the history of salvation that does not have as its necessary instrument the mediation of Our Lady" (Benedict XVI, *Homily*, 11 May 2007).

How great are the wisdom and mercy revealed in this design of God! The most gentle and loving Mary is truly your Mediatrix with God. Whatever God wishes to give you, He first inspires your Mother to ask it of Him—and only then is the grace given, through Her motherly hands and Heart. This truth was understood from the beginning and accepted with the greatest joy by the holy apostles and earliest believers. It was also the belief and teaching of the Fathers of the Church. All the Christian peoples of every age accepted it, and it is only by the greatest violence—and with the most tragic of consequences—that this consoling truth can be uprooted from their hearts, as the history of so many heresies against the Faith of the Church shows us (cf. Leo XIII, *Octobri Mense,* 22 September 1891). It is a truth so important for your soul and for its growth in grace that the whole Church, and especially the holy pontiffs, has repeated it countless times and with infallible certainty.

Our Lady's mediation is truly universal: even when you are unaware of it or cannot remember it, Our Lady is always interceding for you for every grace you receive. God, however, does not want you to be unaware or unmindful of having such a loving Mother and Mediatrix. He wants you to honor your Father *and your Mother*. For this reason there are certain graces He has prepared for you that you cannot receive unless you think of Her and pray to Her expressly; there are certain graces which you cannot receive unless you ask for them explicitly through the Immaculate.

Think about this profound truth and see that it is contained in the Gospel itself: if Our Lady had not been there at Cana in Galilee, Jesus would not then have worked His first miracle. Had the spouses not invited Her to their wedding feast, She would not have obtained this amazing grace for them! This miracle occurred because She was invited, because She interceded, because She spoke to the servants, and because they obeyed Her —and only because She was present and asked for it, did Our Lord anticipate His hour.

If you wish to receive the fullness of grace God has prepared for you from eternity, consecrate yourself to your heavenly Mother. Invite Her and take Her into your home, into your life. Pray to Her, let Her intercede for you, obey Her, and let Her surprise you with Her Motherly love.

Daily Prayers (pp. 79–80)

DAY 8 – THE MAKER OF SAINTS

God desires all men to be saved and to come to the knowledge of truth.

— 1 TIMOTHY 2:4

 alvation is God's will for everyone, and it is God's will for you. And yet, only few reach this goal: "Many are called, few are chosen," Our Lord says (Mt 22:14). And also, "the gate is wide and the way is easy, that leads to destruction, and those who enter by it are many; the gate is narrow and the way is hard, that leads to life, and those who find it are few" (Mt 7:13–15).

Does it not fill your heart with sadness and trepidation to hear the Church mourn how, despite Our Lady's many pleas to us to follow God's will, so many people—so many Catholics—nevertheless go in the direction opposite to the one that leads to salvation? (cf. St. John Paul II, *Homily*, 13 May 1982). Does it not make you serious about how you live your own life? Ask yourself: how do I live my life, my calling to salvation?

So many different sins separate people from God and from one another, taking them in every possible direction away from Him. God's law is broken in so many ways by misguided souls who seek happiness in sin and never find it. Instead of finding it, they are always drifting further from it. So many souls loved by God are lost forever because they refuse to love Him as He wants to be loved, by keeping His commandments. Their sins can be very different, but one thing they all have in common is this: they all lack true devotion to their heavenly Mother. They refuse to hear Her voice saying to them "Do whatever He tells You" (Jn 2:5). They all refuse to take Her into their homes and to be gathered under Her mantle.

The Immaculate Herself wishes to be a safe refuge for all of them: She can never lose grace, and She preserves it for all those who consecrate themselves to Her. Hear Her voice: "He who finds me finds life, and obtains favor from the Lord" (Prv 8:35). Belong to Her then, and rest assured that you will not be lost. Always keep the sobering words of the Church in your heart: "Our Lady foretold and warned us about a way of life that is godless and indeed profanes God in His creatures. Such a life—frequently proposed and imposed—risks leading to hell. We need but take refuge under the protection of the Virgin Mary and to ask Her, as the *Salve Regina* teaches: 'show unto us Jesus'" (Pope Francis, *Homily*, 13 May 2017).

Our Lady is the Mediatrix of every grace for you—its beginning, its growth, its restoration when it is lost, as well as its perfection. Stop and consider all the many saints of the Church—whether those who preserved their innocence since childhood or those who returned to God after a long life of sin—they all loved their Immaculate Mother and let themselves be guided by Her. Wherever She enters, She obtains the grace of conversion and sanctification. The more you belong to Her, the greater will be the work of sanctification that She accomplishes in you.

Jesus will not dwell in souls who reject His Mother. He will not be born in souls in any other way except through Mary Immaculate. Neither will He grow within them, nor make them like Himself, unless it is through Her of whom He Himself was born, through Her at whose side He grew up, through Her who was with Him at the very end of His life. Therefore, even if a soul were to have all other devotions and virtues but not have true devotion to Her, it's devotion is empty and it cannot persevere—its fall is sure.

God has showed you the surest, safest and most beautiful path to saving your soul and becoming a saint. Be consoled therefore and persevere in your resolution to be Hers without limit: it is impossible for anyone who truly belongs to the Immaculate to perish! It is impossible to belong to Her who is full of grace and to live and die without grace.

Daily Prayers (pp. 79–80)

DAY 9 — WORKS OF GRACE AND WORKS OF THE FLESH

My son, give me your heart, and let your eyes observe my ways.
— PROVERBS 23:26

he Church puts these words of Scripture on the holy lips of Our Blessed Mother, who says to us: *Give me your heart, give me your free will, unite your will to mine because I want nothing else for you than the will of my Son, and for this reason I say to you: 'Do whatever He tells you'"* (Jn 2:5).

But remember that either grace or sin can enter through the same heart, that is through free will. If your heart is not consecrated to the Immaculate, sin will enter into it. If you do not live your consecration faithfully—if you do not seek to make every thought, word and action Hers—sin will enter into your thoughts, words, and actions. You must realize your responsibility and choose wisely which desires you allow to enter into your heart.

The human heart cannot serve two masters, and therefore it cannot contain both grace and sin—one is incompatible with the other. Mortal sin (that is any transgression of God's holy law in a grave matter, with full awareness and deliberate consent) repels any and all grace from the heart; whereas venial sin—especially when fully deliberate—stifles that grace and prevents it from accomplishing that for which it was given to you.

You cannot have both grace and sin. Either your heart will love and pursue the works of grace—love, joy, peace, patience, kindness, goodness, faithfulness, gentleness, self-control—or it will love and pursue the works of sin—fornication, impurity, licentiousness, idolatry, sorcery, enmity, strife, jealousy, anger, selfishness, dissension, party spirit, envy, drunkenness, carousing, and the like. If it is works of sin that you still desire, ponder

23

God's holy words to you: whoever does such things cannot enter the Kingdom of God (cf. Gal 5:22).

If you want your heart to belong to Her, you must be ready to battle against your sins: against every mortal sin and deliberate venial sin. Sin is the one thing that Our Lady cannot call Her own and which She cannot offer to God: you must agree to let Her free you from it if you wish to be Hers. Give Her your heart, and She will turn it away from sin.

Do not be afraid or discouraged by the battle you must wage: the Immaculate crushes the head of the lurking serpent by means of resounding victories. She is ready to use you to inflict shattering defeats upon satan if you are ready to fight under Her banner. God has made Her powerful and victorious: She alone suffices for victory—because all other good things come together with Her (cf. Wis 7:11)—and She is *always* victorious!

Daily Prayers (pp. 79–80)

DAY 10 – NEAR OCCASIONS OF SIN

 ince you love God, you must value the priceless gift of sanctifying grace which He bestows upon you, and it must fill you with fear to think that you carry this treasure in a fragile, earthen vessel, always in danger of being broken and lost. Knowing how fragile you are, your mind must be made up to not expose yourself to unnecessary dangers of losing grace.

Every situation in which you are at a high risk of losing grace is called a near occasion of sin. In life, there are very many of these dangerous occasions, and some are unavoidable—we would have to leave this world to be free from all of them! The dangers you cannot avoid are called *necessary* occasions of sin, and those who belong to Our Lady must be confident that this powerful

Mother, victorious over sin, will give them the graces to pass through them unscathed. But there are others that you can and must avoid. A near occasion of sin is called *unnecessary* if you do not have to be in it, but instead you presumptuously choose to put yourself in it anyway.

A near occasion of sin could be a person (who entices you), a place (where there are opportunities to sin) or a thing (an object that you can abuse). Just as you have to avoid sin itself, you have to avoid the unnecessary situations that lead to sin.

The learned saints and Doctors of the Church all tell us: the devil laughs at those who make good resolutions but do not remove themselves from near occasions of sin. The tempter says to them: "Keep doing the things that lead to sin, keep putting yourself in danger, and this time you will not fall into sin, this time it will be different." Do not believe him, it will not be different: as long as you take the path that leads to sin you will end up in sin!

The enemy uses the greatest cunning and care to convince you not to avoid evil occasions, because he knows how these unnecessary occasions stir up your passions and sinful desires within you and make you forget all the good resolutions you had previously made. These occasions are like a veil placed before your eyes, blinding you to the truth God wishes you to remember, and letting you see only the sin right in front of you with all the apparent good and pleasure in it and none of the real evil. In a word: they make you forget all good, and they almost force you into sin. Do you now see why the devil wants you to keep putting yourself in these near occasions?

"Whoever loves danger will perish by it!" (Sir 3:26). Our Lady is always willing to powerfully assist you in every danger—but She cannot help you if you do not want Her help and if you voluntarily expose yourself to the occasion of sin. Remove yourself from all unnecessary, near occasions of sin—whether persons, places, or things. Value the grace that Our Lady has given you, and do not take the risk of losing it. Ask Her to not allow you stray into danger, but to keep you safe under Her mantle, where no evil can harm you.

Daily Prayers (pp. 79–80)

DAY 11 — CONTRITION FOR YOUR SINS AND CONFESSION

To live in total consecration to Our Lady, you must make constant efforts to maintain a clear conscience and to please Her in all you do. The Immaculate cannot have the joy of presenting you to God as Her own if you choose to be in sin.

Although when you are Her possession and property, you can have the greatest confidence that She will help you not to fall into sin, you must nevertheless always remain vigilant. Our Lady will never fail you, but your weakness will remain with you, and—sadly—you will be able to fail Her. If it should happen that your resolve ever grows weak and you fall again, do not delay for a moment to make your return to God. Remember that He has given Our Lady especially to those who are weakest, most miserable, most prone to fall. Pray to Our Lady saying: "Dearest Mother forgive me and obtain forgiveness for me from Jesus." Right then and there, resolve not to sin again. If you turn to Her sincerely and invoke Her with confidence, the Immaculate will not let you sink any deeper. Acknowledge your sin with humility, but make up for it with prompt acts of loving reparation rather than with prolonged sadness. From that very moment, seek to act only for love of Her and Her Son—try to console Her in your very next action by doing whatever Jesus wants of you and doing it as well as possible—and then seek to confess your sin at the next opportunity. If you act this way, rest assured that you will be forgiven by Our Lord and restored to His grace in that very moment.[2]

When you approach the sacrament of confession, do so with great diligence and confidence. Examine your conscience on Calvary together with Mary. At the foot of the cross, She received from Jesus the grace to know each and every child for whom She was suffering, and each and every sin for which She was expiating together with Him. She saw and knew you, and She saw and knew each and every one of your sins. She endured unspeakable suffering because of you, whom She loves so much, because you were the cause of the death of Her Son. She, who knows your soul so intimately, can and will guide you in your examination of conscience if you take the time to recollect yourself in Her loving presence.

When you examine your conscience, think most of all about the fact that it was your fully deliberate sins—whether mortal, or even only venial—which pierced Her Heart most. The Immaculate wants to help you discover your sins—starting with the fully deliberate ones—and to have Her same sentiments of detestation for them. But She does not wish you to remain there: She wants to fill your heart with trust that you can and will overcome them, because She, together with Christ, has had full victory over them.

Your heart must burn with an ardent desire to console your sorrowful Coredemptrix. Yes, She knew you and all your sins which filled Her with bitter grief, but She also knew every sin-

---

2   An act of perfect contrition without a doubt reconciles a soul with God, even before sacramental confession (Cf. Council of Trent). However, *before* does not mean *without*: you must have a sincere resolution of going to confession at your next opportunity. And remember also that **you cannot receive Holy Communion until after the confession has actually taken place.**

cere effort you would make to sin no more. And what an ineffable consolation this was to Her Motherly Heart! Confess your sins frequently and console Her by your profound contrition and firm purpose of amendment in every confession you make.

Daily Prayers (pp. 79–80)

DAY 12 – YOUR GROWTH IN GRACE

o earthly mother can consider her task complete with the birth of her child. She must nourish and educate her child, and God has put into her heart an insuppressible, maternal instinct to do so with the greatest love. And so it is also with the Blessed Virgin Mary's maternal role for each one of Her children. Mary not only gives birth to you, but also nourishes you, raises you and accompanies you for the whole time of your spiritual life—and She does this with the inexpressible love and delight of a true mother.

At the Annunciation, She conceived you as Her child and silently carried you in Her Heart until the moment of Calvary, when Her Maternity was publicly proclaimed by Our Lord to you and to the whole world. Hanging from the Cross, Our Lord did not consider the work of your redemption accomplished until He spoke to His Mother about you: "Behold Your son—because you did not hesitate to offer Me, your only-begotten Son, for a sinner such as this, I give him to You as Your possession and property."

The Church teaches that Our Lady, together with Her Son, possesses true rights over all souls, and therefore over your soul as well. You belong to Her by a true *right of conquest* (cf. Pius XII, *Radio message*, 13 May 1946). This means that together with Jesus and because Jesus wanted it, the Immaculate *paid the price for you to be purchased back from slavery to satan*. The popes and theologians call this the Coredemption: She offered Her Son for your redemption, together with all the pain and sorrow this offering caused Her, and therefore you belong to Her, you are Her possession and property. Jesus gave you to Her, She accepted with love, and She does not want to lose you.

As your Coredemptrix, the Immaculate merited to be proclaimed by Jesus to be your Mother, and the Mother of all mankind, because She participated in the redeeming sacrifice of Her Son in such a special and unique way. She willingly embraced this proclamation with the greatest love and to all its extent. For this reason She does not consider Her task complete after your birth on Calvary: even now She now continues to fulfill Her maternal function from Heaven as the cooperator in the development of divine life in your soul and in the individual souls of all the redeemed.

Do not ever lose heart and do not become discouraged, therefore, if you see yourself sometimes losing grace by sin, sometimes lukewarm and lacking in fervor, sometimes not growing in grace as you would like. She is always your Mother and Her love for you never subsides. She is, moreover, a mother always both willing and able to help you. With Her you will find grace if you lose it, increase in fervor if you have become lukewarm, grow in grace and persevere in it until the end, until you are a saint, the greatest possible saint.

Renew your consecration to Her, tell Her you want to be Hers. Confess your sins frequently and make up for them with redoubled love and zeal—each time converting from sin and turning to God all the more—and you will make rapid progress under Her guidance. She will be more and more a Mother to you, and you will become more and more Her humble, trusting child. The Kingdom of God belongs to such as these.

Daily Prayers (pp. 79–80)

WEEK 2

Take Her into Your Home

DAY 13 – YOUR TRUE MOTHER IN THE ORDER OF GRACE

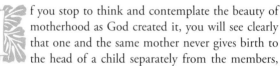f you stop to think and contemplate the beauty of motherhood as God created it, you will see clearly that one and the same mother never gives birth to the head of a child separately from the members, nor to its members separately from the head. Likewise, in the order of grace, the head and the members are born together of the same mother.

In the order of grace, Christ is the Head and all those who are united to Him are called His Mystical Body. Now, Our Lady is the Mother of the *whole Christ*, head and body, not just a part of Him. She is therefore Mother of both the Head of the Mystical Body—Jesus Himself—and of all the members of that Body, the members of the Church, and of you in particular. It follows that the Immaculate became your Mother at the same moment that She became the Mother of Jesus. The Church in fact teaches us that "the two births of the Head and of the Body are distinct but contemporaneous: 'the birth of the Head is the birth of the Body'" (St. Pius X, *Ad diem illum*, 2 February 1904).

Now think carefully about it: if Jesus and you have the same Mother, then you are true brothers. This is what Our Lady's mediation means: She unites God and man, She united Jesus and you, She makes you brothers. She mediates Jesus' very life to you to make you a son of God as He is. You receive no grace without Her! Now, since grace is always a sharing in the divine nature and a participation in the very life of God, if you think about this carefully, you will see the beautiful conclusion easily: Our Lady cannot be for you a Mediatrix of divine life in any other way except by being your Mother. You are united to Jesus and receive God's life in you only through your Mother—just as you receive the life and nature of your earthly father only through your earthly mother.

But there is a great and consoling mystery hidden in this plan of God, which makes Our Lady's Spiritual Maternity even more astoundingly beautiful: whereas your earthly father could not give you his life in any other way except through your mother, your heavenly Father in His omnipotence could have, but *did not want to*. He does not want you to be an orphan and has, therefore, given you a spiritual Mother. For that reason the Church does not ever hesitate to say and repeat: "We cannot be Christian without being Marian!" (St. Paul VI, *Homily*, 24 April 1970).

The Church teaches that this most consoling truth which, by the free choice of God the All-Wise, is an integrating part of the mystery of human salvation, and therefore it must be held with divine Faith by all Christians (cf. St. Paul VI, *Signum Magnum*, 13 May 1967). Take this truth to heart, hold and profess it with your whole being, and be consoled to be a true child of God and a true child of Mary!

Daily Prayers (pp. 81–82)

DAY 14 — YOUR TOTAL DEPENDENCE ON MARY

he Immaculate is far more a Mother to you than even your earthly mother is, because you depend on Her far more than you do on your mother on earth. In fact, you depend on Her at every single moment of your spiritual life, for every grace and every time, without exception.

Things are not the same with spiritual life as they are with biological life. A baby, once born, could live its own life without its earthly mother as a little orphan (if, for example, a heroic mother must lay down her life in the delivery of her child, as many saintly mothers have done). But you cannot live your spiritual life without your heavenly Mother even for one instant. This is so because She is mediating to you the grace you need to be a child of God at every instant, and, without Her, God will not give His grace to anyone. If, therefore, your soul ever breaks its union with Her, it ceases to live.

Think for a moment that if you were to wish to leave Her, and if She were to let you go from Her immaculate hands even for an instant, you would immediately fall into sin, and the most grievous of sins. Without Her, you would have nowhere to go except away from God, your source of Divine Life, until you saw yourself eternally separated from Him in the depths of hell. The mere thought of this possibility should fill your soul with dread and make you turn to Her to plead for help, as the holy children of Fatima did when they were permitted to see hell, where the souls of poor sinners go. It is to save them—to save you—that God wishes to establish devotion to His Immaculate Mother in the world. She will never let go of you for a single moment if you turn to Her always!

Unite your soul to Hers and let nothing separate you from Her. Once you learn to keep your soul attached to your heavenly Mother by continual recourse and prayer, you have grasped the secret and the fundamental condition of the spiritual life. Take comfort in knowing that you can be Hers always and everywhere, because nothing outside of you will ever be able to separate you from your heavenly Mother: neither tribulation, nor distress, nor persecution, nor famine, nor nakedness, nor peril, nor the sword; neither death, nor life, nor angels, nor principalities, nor things present, nor things to come, nor powers, nor height, nor depth, nor anything else in all creation.

Only your free will and a deliberate decision to sin could ever separate you from the Immaculate. Your free will is such a great power and yet such a great weakness: it can unite you to Her, or it can separate you. Can you possibly trust yourself to always use your free will wisely? Do as the saints did and put no trust in yourself, but pray to Her that She will disregard your free will if you were to try to abuse it to sin against God. And if you were ever to try to break loose from Her immaculate hands, pray that She might force you—even if it hurts and even if you protest—that unheeding of any of your resistance, She might all the more press you close to Her Heart.

Daily Prayers (pp. 81–82)

DAY 15 – KNOW YOUR MOTHER

Mary, your heavenly Mother, knows you and She knows you perfectly, because She sees you in the Beatific Vision of God in Heaven. She is not unaware of you and you are very much on Her mind, even at this very moment. In contemplating God, everything that concerns Her as the Mother of men and Mediatrix of All Graces is revealed by Him to Her. God Himself shares His own knowledge with Her so that nothing that Her motherly Heart must know about you remains hidden from Her.

Because your Mother knows and loves you and never stops thinking of you, you must honor Her by frequently thinking of Her and returning Her love. Now, you cannot love without knowing, and you cannot know without learning. For this reason, you cannot respond to Her love for you without making efforts to learn about Her.

To learn about Her, you must read about Her in good books, hear about Her in devout sermons and retreats. You must study Her presence and action in the lives of the saints and in their writings. It is good to read books, especially those written by saints, and not only once, but multiple times, meditating them over and over again. St. Louis de Montfort himself acknowledged that he did not understand many of the things he wrote, which means that he did so under the inspiration of Our Lady. It means also that She Herself will reveal hidden things to those who devoutly read what She inspired Her servants to write. St. Maximilian, moreover, never tired of repeating that the vast depths of the mystery of the Immaculate Conception still remain largely hidden and will only be revealed to those who humbly search and pray for understanding.

You must remember, however, that the first and most essential thing in seeking to know the Immaculate is profound humility. Humility means you must realize who you are and who She is. You, a sinner—She, the Immaculate One, without blemish, without any sin. If you stand before Her as an unworthy sinner, confident in Her goodness and not in your own—only then can you hope to obtain the grace of knowing Her and loving Her. "God opposes the proud, but gives grace to the humble" (1Pt 5:5).

When you read about Her, always remember that you are coming into contact with a living Person. Lift up your mind and pray to Her during your studies. Mortify your curiosity from things that only distract you and do not help you to know Her —such penance purifies the mind and heart to make them able to see and understand with greater clarity.

And whenever your mind does not understand, study more, pray more, and never tire of it. Consult learned persons and devout servants of the Immaculate, but, above all, turn to Her with your questions and ask for enlightenment, and She Herself will give you the knowledge that leads to love.

Daily Prayers (pp. 81–82)

DAY 16 — PRAY TO YOUR MOTHER

Pray that you may not enter into temptation...
pray always without becoming weary.

— LUKE 22:40; 18:1

t every moment of your life, you can choose to be faithful or unfaithful to grace, to be fervent, lukewarm or cold; you must choose either to accept grace from Our Lady, or to refuse it. You cannot predetermine your free will ahead of time, and your many failures to carry out your good resolutions are proof of this. Like everyone else, you must persevere until the end by continuous prayer, incessantly asking for perseverance in doing good and avoiding evil, always asking and receiving from the Immaculate the graces you need for each moment of life. The grace you need to be saved and sanctified—especially final perseverance—cannot be merited, and so must be obtained by prayer.

Think: one sin is enough to condemn even a saint. You must therefore be on your guard to never fall into presumption and never take your final perseverance for granted. But know also and be sure that one act of repentance is enough to justify even the greatest sinner, and for this reason you should never despair for yourself or for anyone else.

To remain faithful to God's grace in every circumstance of life, seek to enter into true communion of soul with the Immaculate, and to remain in such constant union by incessant prayer. Never cease to tell your Mother what is happening around you and inside of you, and your whole life will become a prayer to Her. Remember Her presence and consult Her in all your actions, turn to Her in all your difficulties and perplexities, surrender all your anxieties to Her. Unite yourself to Her in all the countless emotions of your soul, whether good or bad, pleasant or painful. Tell Her not only your profound emotions but even the simple impressions and reflections which your ordinary occupations suggest. Do not all children feel the need to share their experiences with their mothers? And are you not truly Her child, and She your Mother? If you truly believe this, as you must, then live your life accordingly!

There is only one sure sign of your perseverance in grace and future holiness, and it is continual union with Our Lady by prayer. Will you be faithful to prayer? Or will you continue to neglect it? This very moment, break the habit of putting off your true conversion until a tomorrow that never comes and turn to the Immaculate with Saint Alphonsus, saying: "My dearest Mother, *give me* the will to pray to you always. I know that You are very good, so good that if You were to see me culpably neglect prayer, You would force me to pray just to not see me lost." Continual recourse to Our Lady is the sum and conclusion of the whole theology of this great Doctor of the Church.

What an important truth for us! Our eternal salvation and sanctification depend on continual recourse to our spiritual Mother, from whom we receive all grace from God. How you should thank God for giving you such a beautiful and easy way of saving your soul and even becoming a saint, a great saint. How you should desire to pray to Her always and develop this habit during your life, so that you might practice it also at the moment of your death!

Daily Prayers (pp. 81–82)

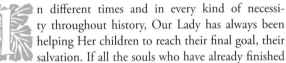

DAY 17 — ASK HER FOR GRACE AND YOU WILL RECEIVE IT

In different times and in every kind of necessity throughout history, Our Lady has always been helping Her children to reach their final goal, their salvation. If all the souls who have already finished their earthly pilgrimage could speak, countless volumes could be written about the wonders of grace that this loving Mother has accomplished in their lives. But even these many volumes would contain only a small fraction of the tender care of this good Mother for Her children. This is so because *all graces* come to us from Her, even those we are unaware of—and just think of how often the Immaculate needs to intervene for you without you even realizing the dangers you are in.

In recent times, Our Lady has given to the world a tangible reminder of Her universal mediation of grace: the Miraculous Medal. She Herself appeared to St. Catherine Labouré in a supernatural vision, showing her the pattern of the medal and asking that it be struck accordingly, as seen by the Saint. To all who would wear it around their neck, Our Lady promised special graces and blessings, and history quickly proved how true Our Lady's promise was, meriting for the medal the name "miraculous."

On this medal, Our Lady's hands are open and luminous rays of light effuse from rings on Her fingers, to show the world that

God wants to give grace, and He wants to give it through Mary. But not all the rings give off this splendid light: some give none. When St. Catherine Labouré asked Our Lady the meaning of this detail of the holy vision, She explained to her that there are some graces that She never dispenses because no one asks for them. The rings that give no light symbolize riches of grace that never reach the souls for whom they are destined, because these souls do not pray for them. Our Lady always has graces available to you for all your necessities, but She is unable to give them to you if She does not hear you asking for them and desiring them. You must, therefore, ask for them with confidence and trust— both for yourself and for others.

Wear the Miraculous Medal with faith and share it with others. Learn and pray the simple prayer Our Lady has taught us: "O Mary conceived without sin, pray for us who have recourse to You." Pray it for yourself and for others, especially those who most need grace and mercy: for the Freemasons and all other enemies of the Church, for heretics and for schismatics and for all those who are in any way far from God. This good Mother can work miracles of grace if only a person accepts Her medal and agrees to wear it. The least bit of good will is sufficient for Our Lady to enter a soul and to shower it with grace and blessings that surpass all expectation.

The Church, therefore, does not hesitate to apply to the Blessed Virgin Mary the words of Scripture: "Happy is the man who listens to me, watching daily at my gates, waiting beside my doors. For he who finds me finds life, and obtains favor from the Lord" (Prv 8:34–35).

Pray to Her often and see how true God's Word is: "*All good things came to me along with Her, and in Her hands uncounted wealth*" (Wis 7:11).

Daily Prayers (pp. 81–82)

DAY 18 – LOVE HER ROSARY AND PRAY IT EVERY DAY

ur Lady loves to hear Her children recite the prayer of the Holy Rosary, and in Her many apparitions She has asked us repeatedly to pray it every day. In Lourdes in a particular way Our Blessed Mother showed Her special love for this prayer. While Bernadette prayed the Rosary during Our Lady's apparition, kneeling before Her in the grotto, She lovingly listened and ran Her own fingers through the beads, reciting the *Glory be* together with the little Saint.

Think deeply and realize what God wishes to teach you by this apparition of His Mother praying the Rosary with St. Bernadette: to enter deeply into the mysteries of the life of Jesus, from His conception all the way until the moment He crowned His Mother Queen, you must contemplate these mysteries with Mary, saying and repeating the "Hail Mary." You must recall and meditate on these mysteries with Her, who was the first to have already pondered them in Her own Heart. During the earthly life of Her Son, She saw Him and often spoke with Him, and after His Ascension, She continued to ponder everything in Her Heart until Her own Assumption into Heaven. All the meditations you can make now about Jesus were already made by Her long ago. If you meditate with Her now She will guide you to understand, feel, and long for what She understood, felt, and longed for. She will share Her own experiences with you, and you will see Jesus through Her eyes and love Him with Her Heart. Do you realize now why the Immaculate hopes in a very special way to see you pray the Rosary daily? She wants to teach you and form you by this prayer. Therefore, if you wish to belong to Our Lady totally and be molded by Her as Her possession and property, you must love Her Rosary and pray it every day.

The Church wishes you to be aware that if you want to know Jesus and love Him profoundly, you must study Him and His mysteries in the school of Mary (cf. St. John Paul II, *Rosarium Virginis Mariae*, 16 October 2002). No one in the world knew Jesus as She did, and, hence, no one is a better teacher and guide for making Jesus known; no one is equal to Her in uniting us to Jesus (St. Pius X, *Ad diem illum*, 2 February 1904). From the frequent meditation on the mysteries of the life of Jesus and Mary, your soul will little by little, and without you even noticing it, absorb the virtues they contain; you will be enkindled with a longing for things immortal and more easily impelled to follow the path which Christ Himself and His Mother have followed. The recitation of identical formulas, repeated so many times—rather than making your prayer sterile and boring—will, on the contrary, arouse confidence in your weary heart and bear a gentle compulsion on the motherly Heart of your Mother (cf. Pius XII, *Ingruentorum Malorum*, 15 September 1951).

The Holy Rosary is an easy way to be united to the Immaculate, to ask Her for grace, to be taught by Her, transformed by Her into Christ. If you say the Rosary every day you can be sure that despite the gravity of your sins, you will receive a never-fading crown of glory (1 Pt 5:4). Even if you are now lukewarm and lacking in fervor, or, worse still, even if you are struggling with mortal sin and on the brink of damnation, even if you have one foot in hell, even if you have wandered from the true Faith, or are bound by addictions and bad habits, even if you have gone so far as to have sold your soul to the devil—sooner or later you will be set free, amend your life and save your soul, if you say the Holy Rosary devoutly every day until death, for the purpose of knowing the truth and obtaining contrition and pardon for your sins.

Will you begin to pray the Rosary today? Or, if you already pray it, will you make the effort to pray it better, with greater reverence, attention, and devotion?

Daily Prayers (pp. 81–82)

DAY 19 – LET HER FEED YOU AND NOURISH YOU

ince the Immaculate is your true Mother, She must raise you, educate you, form you and make you like Jesus in all things. Her maternal mission is to gradually teach you to think, feel, will, and act like Him. More truly than St. Paul, She can say about you: "My little child, with whom I am again in travail until Christ be formed in you!" (Gal 4:19).

She will form you to the full stature of Christ in a particularly efficacious manner by the grace of graces, the source and summit of our Faith, the most Holy Eucharist, in which Jesus Himself is truly present with His body, blood, soul and divinity. You must let yourself be nourished by your Mother by means of worthy and devout reception of this holiest of sacraments.

Be aware that Our Lady wants to be with you in a special way when you receive the Most Blessed Sacrament. At every Holy Communion you receive, it is quite correct to say that there is a holy, sweet and mysterious presence of Mary, inseparably and totally united with Jesus in the Host. This is so because the body and blood of Jesus, present under the appearances of bread and wine in the Eucharist, were received by Him entirely from the body and blood of Mary. The Eucharist is the Bread of the Mother of God, our Mother. Every mother nourishes her child with her own substance, first when the child is still in her womb by her own blood and then after its birth with her milk. The same is true for Mary, and for this reason we can say that the Eucharist is the Bread made by Mary from the flour of Her immaculate flesh and blood, kneaded with Her virginal milk. It is Bread with which She wishes to nourish you. That is why the Church, in adoring Our Lord in the Eucharist, never ceases to proclaim Him to be the Son of Mary, saying *Ave Verum Corpus Natum de Maria Virgine*—Hail True Body, Born of the Virgin Mary (cf. St. John Paul II, *Angelus*, 5 June 1983).

Show yourself grateful for this precious gift your loving Mother wants to give to you. Be sure to never abuse the Sacrament of the Eucharist by sacrilegious Communion in the state of mortal sin. The Church teaches the faithful that for no crime is there heavier punishment to be feared from God than for the unholy or irreligious use of the Eucharist, which contains the very Author and Source of Holiness (*The Catechism of the Council of Trent*).

Our Lady can nourish your soul only if it is alive. If it is dead in sin, She first wants to lead you to forgiveness and new life in the sacrament of confession, where you meet your loving and merciful Redeemer, always willing to forgive and restore you to His friendship. Receive therefore only when you are in the state of grace! And if you were to ever lose grace, make sure to first have recourse to confession to be forgiven and restored to it before receiving Communion.

Oh, how your Mother wishes you to grow in devotion to the Eucharist! Even if your soul is already adorned with grace, do not neglect to prepare for Communion by increasing your fervor and welcoming Our Lord with the greatest love possible. Do not receive Him into a heart that is alive, but indifferent and unwelcoming. If you are faithful in receiving worthily and devoutly, Our Lady will constantly deepen your relations with Jesus in His Sacrament of love. Receive Jesus in Holy Communion as if it were Our Lady Herself giving Him to you. Receive not out of routine, vainglory, or any other human motive, but with an attentive faith, an ardent desire to be healed by this divine medicine, and to be transformed by Our Lady into Him whom you receive.

Daily Prayers (pp. 81–82)

WEEK 3
Become Like Your Mother

No one can serve two masters; for either he will hate the one and love the other, or he will be devoted to the one and despise the other.

— MATTHEW 6:24

You cannot love the Immaculate and love to live in sin at the same time. Loving Her means hating sin. Loving sin means hating Her.

Your Baptism has made you a child of God and a child of Mary. It has freed you from sin and servitude to satan. It has separated you from the world, and you no longer belong to it. For this reason the Holy Spirit says to you: "Do not love the world or the things in the world. If anyone loves the world, love for the Father is not in him. For all that is in the world, the lust of the flesh and the lust of the eyes and the pride of life, is not of the Father but is of the world" (1Jn 2:15–16). Your consecration to Our Blessed Lady would not be pleasing to God or to Her if it were *worldly*, that is if it did not entail a battle against the world and an effort to live a holy life. It would be a false consecration and a false devotion.

Our Blessed Lady wishes you to live your consecration to Her in the world, but She does not wish you to be *of the world*. Do not try to conceal wordly behaviors like pride, selfishness, greed, lust, drunkenness, anger, swearing, gossip, slandering, injustice and other vices under the name and the appearance of belonging to the Immaculate. Your actions must agree with your words: your formula of consecration to Our Lady cannot hide your sinful actions from the eyes of God. Do not deceive yourself and think that because you have given yourself to Our Blessed Mother, you are somehow entitled to love the world without regret and expect to be forgiven anyway. Do not live peacefully in your wicked habits, without making any effort to correct them, believing that your consecration to Our Lady gives you this kind of liberty. Do not fool yourself into thinking that you can mock God, that He will forgive such presumptuous sins, and that you will not die without confession and not be lost for all eternity.

To truly belong to Our Lady, it is necessary to be genuinely determined to avoid all mortal sin and deliberate venial sin, as well as to practice self-discipline in order to avoid sin and unnecessary occasion of sin. Consecration to Her requires doing "violence" to yourself, overpowering the evil desires of your fallen nature by the grace of the Spirit, for as the Lord says, "the kingdom of heaven suffers violence, and the violent are taking it by force" (Mt 11:12).

Our Lady wants to set you free from slavery to the sins the world loves. Remember always: there is one thing that cannot belong to Her or become Her property, and that is sin. Resolve to tirelessly fight against it and implore Her help. She wants You to belong to Her, not to the world, and to experience the freedom of the children of God. She is able to convert even the most lukewarm soul and the most hardened sinner. Should you be such a one—lukewarm or struggling with mortal sin —know that She is the Mother of the Almighty God, greater than your greatest sins. As long as you persevere in your sincere efforts, She will obtain for you the grace to no longer live complacently in the state of sin, but to repent and to be pardoned, to overcome your evil habits, and to grow in grace until you reach the fullness of grace to which you are called by God.

Daily Prayers (pp. 83–84)

DAY 21 — A FIRM RESOLUTION TO IMITATE THE IMMACULATE

ou cannot become holy in an instant and without effort. You must slowly take on the virtues of Our Lady in order to become the saint you are called to be. Acts of virtue require repetition until they become your stable pattern of conduct, until vice is fully extirpated. You must get used to trying over and over again until your whole pattern of conduct becomes virtuous and holy, until you become firmly established in doing good and avoiding evil.

Once you are consecrated to the Immaculate, you will not become like Her instantly—your many bad habits will remain for you to contend with, and you will have to work to replace them with the virtues of Our Lady. Therefore do not be surprised that, even when you already belong to Her, initially you will still fall. But be sure that you will do so less frequently, less grievously, and you will get up more promptly, overcome temptation more readily, persevere more surely.

Belonging to the Immaculate means constant effort to act like Her, speak like Her, think like Her, trying again and again without growing discouraged. You must perseveringly try until you succeed, knowing that Our Lady is pleased with you because of every sincere effort you make, even if those efforts frequently fail and you remain unhappy with yourself.

The true sorrow with which Our Lady wishes to fill your soul does not consist in dwelling on your unhappiness with yourself, or on being sad or discouraged, but rather in a firm resolution to turn back to your Mother with all the more trust, seeking all the more to please Her in your very next action. Our Lady is able to sanctify you more than you are able to sin, and for this reason you must never become disheartened. As long as your mind remains firmly made up and your efforts are unwavering, Our Lady will make you a saint. Even if your sins seem to persist and you think they will not go away, if you continue to have recourse to Her, She will lead you to victory. She will give you Her virtues—especially Her humility—and you will slowly imitate them all and reproduce them within yourself.

Like a child who runs to its mother in all that happens to it, good or evil, so you must constantly run to Her. Pray to Her always with your lips and with your thoughts, and you will experience in yourself how the Immaculate will take ever greater possession of your soul, how your belonging to Her will deepen more and more in every way. You will notice that your faults will weaken and vanish, as She gently and powerfully draws you closer and closer to Herself.

Daily Prayers (pp. 83–84)

DAY 22 – YOUR DUTIES IN LIFE ARE HER WILL FOR YOU

 he Church teaches us that it looks to Mary as its model, because it sees in Her—without spot or wrinkle—all the perfection to which it is called. The Church turns its eyes to Mary who shines forth to the whole community of the elect as the model of virtues (cf. II Council of the Vatican, *Lumen Gentium* 65).

She is a true model, but not a merely passive one. She is a living model, a motherly model, a teacher of virtue. Everything about Her life is a lesson for you. Consequently you cannot fail to carefully study and meditate on Her life and to notice how most of it is hidden, lived quietly at the side of Jesus in the holy house of Nazareth. You must study and imitate Her even in this hidden life of Hers, which occupied most of Her time here on earth.

By Her quiet fidelity to the duties of Her life—unnoticed by the world but noticed by God—She is for you an admirable example of how to reach holiness by faithfulness to your own duties, especially the hidden ones, which God alone sees. The Church teaches us to not overlook the wonders God performed in the hiddenness of the life of the Immaculate: "Let us remember that the perfection of Mary, full of grace, is proclaimed by the angel within the walls of Her home—not in Nazareth's main square, but there, in hiding, in the greatest humility… God wants to do great things with us in our daily lives: that is, in our families, at work, in everyday environments. God's grace loves to operate there more than in great historical events" (Pope Francis, *Angelus*, 8 December 2021).

If your desire to belong to Our Lady is authentic, you must wish to be sanctified the same way She was, that is in your ordinary life. Do not expect your heavenly Mother to obtain great graces for you if you refuse to accept the little ones. "He who is faithful in a very little is faithful also in much; and he who is dishonest in a very little is dishonest also in much" (Lk 16:10). Do not expect to become a saint if you fail to give yourself wholeheartedly to fulfilling your obligations out of love for Our Lady: duties in your family, in your workplace, at school, in church, etc.

Consecration to the Immaculate elevates you and sanctifies you in the very state of life you are in—single, married or consecrated to God—with all its obligations and duties to God and neighbor, big and small. But no state in life, not even the holiest, is a guarantee of sanctity if you neglect the duties of that state. In these duties, you must see the sure will of the Immaculate for you. In their fulfillment you must see the test of your love for Her, and, through Her, for God. She will not be pleased with even the holiest actions you might perform—such as prayer and penance—if these are an obstacle to the fulfillment of your duties.

Seek therefore not to do extraordinary things out of a disguised self-love, but be faithful to your ordinary duties out of authentic love for Her. Never forget that holiness does not consist of extraordinary actions, but ordinary, often unnoticed actions, done out of love for your Father who sees in secret. This is how the Immaculate lived and so you must live also, if you wish to be truly Hers!

Daily Prayers (pp. 83–84)

DAY 23 – IMITATE HER MODESTY AND PURITY

y your consecration to the Immaculate, your soul with all its faculties and your body with all its senses will belong to Her. If the body of all those who are baptized is a temple of the Holy Spirit, think of how much more gladly the Spirit will dwell in the body of those who have consecrated themselves without reserve to His Beloved Spouse! "Do you not know that your body is a temple of the Holy Spirit within you, which you have from God? You are not your own; you were bought with a price. So glorify God in your body" (1 Cor 6:19–20). Resolve to show that you belong to the Immaculate by glorifying God in your body, that is by your pure and modest conduct, by the way you act and, also, by the way you dress. "Let your modesty be known to all men" (Phil 4:4–5)—be modest in the choice of clothing with which you veil and dignify your body.

Protect the dignity of your person by not allowing yourself to be objectified by others. Our Lord says to you: "Do not throw your pearls before swine, lest they trample them under foot and turn to attack you" (Mt 7:6). Realize that if you do not value your dignity and purity—if you do not command respect for yourself by your modest clothing and chaste conduct—both will be taken from you. You will not receive respect: instead you will be objectified, trampled by the lustful minds of persons who do not care about you, but are like swine that attack and tear to pieces. Your dignity is so great and precious that if you allow it to be taken away, you grieve the Holy Spirit of God and sin gravely: "Put off your old nature which belongs to your former manner of life and is corrupt through deceitful lusts, and be renewed in the spirit of your minds, and put on the new nature, created after the likeness of God in true righteousness and holiness [and] do not grieve the Holy Spirit of God" (Eph 4:22–24.30).

Because you belong to the Immaculate totally, your eyes, your mind, and your thoughts also belong to Her. Therefore view others with purity too—do not objectify them by lust. Do not be like swine that do not value, but only trample the pearls placed before them. "Everyone who looks at a woman lustfully has already committed adultery with her in his heart. If your right eye causes you to sin, pluck it out and throw it away; it is better that you lose one of your members than that your whole body be thrown into hell" (Mt 5:28–29). Cut yourself off from whatever leads you to the sin of lust, rather than seeing yourself cut off from grace and to fall into sin. If you faithfully maintain the purity of your eyes, one day they will behold Our Lady in Heaven.

Modesty means "refusing to unveil what should remain hidden. Modesty is decency. It inspires one's choice of clothing. Modesty inspires a way of life which makes it possible to resist the allurements of fashion and the pressures of prevailing ideologies" (*Catechism of the Catholic Church*, 2521–2523). "Certain fashions will be introduced which will greatly offend Our Lord." Will you allow these words of Our Lady, spoken to St. Jacinta of Fatima, to speak to you as well? Or will you resist grace and continue to tell yourself your clothing is modest, even if it unveils and draws attention to what does not belong for the public to see? Even if you know you are allowing yourself to be objectified? Will you continue to objectify and take with your lustful mind what does not belong to you?

Our Lady loves the virtue of purity, and She wants to adorn you with it, but you must pray earnestly to Her to receive and live it faithfully. It will set you free, restore your dignity, and give you a peace that the world cannot give, transcending even that which it can imagine (cf. Phil 4:6).

Daily Prayers (pp. 83–84)

DAY 24 – LOVE THOSE SHE LOVES AND AS SHE LOVES

 efore you can make the gift of yourself to the Immaculate, your heart must be free from indifference and especially from any ill will or unforgiveness towards your neighbor: "If you are offering your gift at the altar, and there remember that your brother has something against you, leave your gift there before the altar and go; first be reconciled to your brother, and then come and offer your gift" (Mt 5:23–24). Forgive from the heart all those who have wronged you, ask forgiveness of those whom you have wronged. Ask Our Lady to use you for the good of all souls, even those who have hurt you and those whom you do not know, and show yourself zealous for their happiness, salvation and sanctification. Examine your heart and make sure it is not indifferent or even closed to anyone so loved by Our Lady.

The Immaculate is a Mother who is all goodness, all tenderness, all mercy—and think how fortunate you are to personally experience Her Motherly goodness to you. The very thought of Her unconditional love for you can so effectively drive away sadness and dejection from your heart, giving you hope and anchoring you to Her regardless of any storms you might be going through! How consoling it should be for you to know that the mere invocation of Her Name "Mary" resonates profoundly in Her loving Heart, always ready to listen to you, especially when you are in darkness, dryness or even in the unhappy situation of sin. And the more unhappy you are—even if you have had the misfortune of committing sin—the more She tries to envelop you within Her loving mantle.

It is with the same love She has for you that She also loves all your brothers and sisters in Christ. And because She loves them, you too must love them, and lead them to their heavenly Mother. Recall your own experience: have you not noticed an astonishing transformation in yourself since you began to pray to the Immaculate? You have been given a light to guide you from the darkness of your sins, do not hide it under a bushel basket, but make it shine before others.

Do you not wish for as many souls as possible to come to experience this same love that their Mother has for them? And can you possibly be unmoved at the thought of the joy you can bring to your heavenly Mother by bringing to Her all Her scattered, lonely, and sad children whom you meet, and allow Her to bestow love upon each of them? Think of how many souls—even good Christian souls—do not know their Mother, and are without Her consolation in life. You cannot be indifferent to so many children She loves so dearly, for whom She suffered together with Jesus. The grace of total consecration to the Immaculate which you have received is a gift that you must share with those who are still without it.

This is how the Immaculate wants you to love, according to Her Son's new commandment: "Love one another, even as I have loved you" (Jn 13:34). If you wish to be Hers, you must love your neighbor, and you must love him as you love yourself. And even more than this: you must love your neighbor as Christ loves him.

The thought of so many unhappy souls who neither know Her nor Her Son, who do not know how loved they are by Jesus and Mary, must urge you on to work for their salvation and sanctification by means of the apostolate. Let Her use you as She wishes to bring souls to Her, and through Her to Jesus. Jesus Christ is the only Mediator between God and humanity, the Immaculate is the only Mediatrix between humanity and Jesus, and you can be a happy mediator between Her and so many needy souls scattered throughout the world.

Daily Prayers (pp. 83–84)

DAY 25 – TRANSUBSTANTIATION INTO THE IMMACULATE[3]

he Immaculate belongs to God in the most perfect and ineffable way. To express just how closely God united Her to Himself, it is not exaggerated to use an expression found in the writings of the Fathers and theologians—and approved by the Church—and to say that She is a complement (or "completion") of the Trinity. This means that none of the Divine Persons of the Trinity will enter into communion with anyone outside of the Trinity without Her—neither Father, nor Son, nor Holy Spirit, will share Their divine life with creation without the collaboration of Our Lady. For this reason, without Our Blessed Lady, our knowledge and

---

3   Saint Maximilian loves to use the word "transubstantiation" to express the totality of our spiritual transformation into the Immaculate. We must remember, however, that he uses this term analogously. Christians cannot be literally "transubstantiated" into Our Blessed Lady, and, no matter how perfect our transformation into Her, no real change of substance will occur. We will never literally become the same person as the Immaculate. When we properly understand the analogy St. Maximilian is employing, we can better understand his frequent exhortation to "devote ourselves to Her completely without any limitation … so as to become, somehow, Herself living, speaking, acting in this world" (*Letter*, 28 February 1933).

participation of the life of the Holy Trinity remains always partial and incomplete.

The relationship of Our Lady with the Holy Trinity surpasses that of any other creature, human or angelic. Though She is not a divine person Herself, yet She has a sublime relationship with each of Them. She is the Beloved Daughter and handmaid of the Father, the true Mother of the Son, and the inseparable Spouse of the Holy Spirit. She is the possession and property of God in a way far superior to all other creatures. For this reason, She also enjoys the greatest possible degree of intimacy with God.

If you become truly Hers, She will introduce you too into an inexpressible intimacy with the Most Holy Trinity—and you will belong to God in the most perfect way possible. She will then love God through you and in you in the most perfect way. With your poor miserable heart, She will love God and you will become the means by which the Immaculate Herself loves God. And God—seeing that you are Her property, Her possession, almost a part of Her, almost His very dearly beloved Mother Herself—will love Her in you. What sublime mysteries you are a part of!

You have heard of unfortunate persons who have suffered diabolical possession, persons through whom the devil thought, spoke and acted. Those who consecrate themselves to Our Lady must wish to be possessed in this same way, but *by Her, by the Immaculate*—to be unlimitedly possessed by Her so that She Herself might freely think, speak and act through them. You must desire to be Hers to the point that nothing of your own remains, to be changed into Her, transubstantiated into Her so that She alone remains, so that God sees nothing in you that is not Hers. And then, seeing only Her, God will admit you to wondrous intimacy with Himself, with each of the Persons of the Holy Trinity.

Think of the great joy you will bring to the Heart of God when

He sees you surrendering yourself to Her totally and letting Her freely act in you, and through Her belonging to Him perfectly, just as She did. Your sole desire, therefore, must be to be perfectly like Her—transubstantiated into Her—and to belong perfectly to Her, just as She belongs perfectly to God.

Daily Prayers (pp. 83–84)

DAY 26 – CONVERT AGAIN AND AGAIN

ransubstantiation into the Immaculate[4] does not happen instantly as does Eucharistic transubstantiation. It is often slow and laborious, and comes at the price of great efforts made for love of Our Lady. Even though not every effort of yours might be successful —even though you might fail often—Our Lady's patience will never run out for you as you constantly try to rise from sin to grace, to resist tepidity and to gradually increase from grace to more and more grace. The Church looks to Mary, and "it sees Her helping the Christian people in the constant struggle between good and evil, to ensure that they 'do not fall' or, if they have fallen, that they will 'rise again'" (St. John Paul II, *Redemptoris Mater*, 25 March 1987).

To be transformed into Her, the Immaculate wants you to make frequent use of the sacrament of confession (which is also called the sacrament of penance) because Christ Her Son instituted it for you. For this reason, you cannot neglect this sacrament, but you must rather receive it often. Do not think you do not need confession! Even if, by the grace of God, you are free from mortal sin, do not fool yourself into thinking that you can remain free for long if you habitually neglect confession. Remember that by receiving the sacrament of penance frequently, you

---

4   See footnote 3, Day 25.

are prevented from falling back into mortal sin; every time you make your confession, the sacramental grace you receive converts you more and more firmly from sin to God, and keeps you steadfastly converted to Him. Your venial sins also become less and less deliberate and your thirst for greater holiness increases steadily.

Do you value this sacrament as you should? Do you prepare diligently for it by praying to know your sins? Do you examine your conscience thoroughly and confess your sins humbly and sincerely? Is your purpose of amendment firm and concrete every time you confess your sins, especially when they are frequently repeated, and even if they are merely venial? Do you fervently fulfill the penance imposed upon you?

The Holy Spirit inspired the practice of frequent confession in the Church, as the popes teach us, and it is for this reason that Our Lady, the Spouse of the Holy Spirit, wishes you to follow this inspiration. By frequent confession, you become more docile to the same Holy Spirit and His fruits are formed in you. To ensure more rapid progress day by day in the path of virtue, frequent reception of the sacrament of confession should become a part of your life. By the grace of sacramental absolution your attachment to sin will weaken, your possession of grace will intensify; your self-knowledge will increase, and Christian humility will grow in you; you will correct bad habits and resist spiritual negligence and tepidity; your conscience will be purified, your will strengthened, and you will attain self-control and dominion over your senses and passions (Pius XII, *Mystici Corporis*, 29 June 1943). Be sincere in your resolve to be guided and transformed by the Immaculate, and do not fail to often approach the sacrament of penance, so as to reap its fruits of grace.

Daily Prayers (pp. 83–84)

WEEK 4
Let Yourself Be Guided by Her

DAY 27 – THE SPOUSE OF THE HOLY SPIRIT

 hen in Lourdes St. Bernadette Soubirous asked Our Lady to reveal Her Name, Our Lady opened Her clasped hands and extended them to the ground. Then, lifting them up again, She joined them as in prayer, and, gazing toward Heaven with inexpressible gratitude, She finally said to Bernadette: "*I am the Immaculate Conception.*" It was the first time in her life that this simple young girl had heard these words. She did not understand their meaning, which is why she tried not to forget them, and repeated them her whole way home until she dutifully communicated them to her parish priest.

Our Lady loves the name She revealed to Bernadette, because it expresses a very special and completely unique privilege She received from the Most High God: She alone can call Herself *the Immaculate Conception*. But this name also contains a hidden mystery: Our Lady's ineffable union with the Holy Spirit as His Spouse. The Holy Spirit, in fact, is also an Immaculate Conception, but uncreated and eternal, within the Trinity. His "conception" is an eternal spiration—it is the very same as His procession from the Father and the Son from all eternity. The Holy Spirit is the uncreated *Immaculate Conception*; Our Lady, the created *Immaculate Conception*.

Think: Our Lady and the Holy Spirit share the same name! What does this mean? It means that they are united by a very close bond. A bond so close that we must speak of it as of a spousal union. If among human beings a bride receives the name of her husband—because she belongs to him, she unites herself to him, she becomes like him and together with him she becomes a creative agent of new life—how much more does this happen with the Immaculate and the Holy Spirit? The name of Him who is the uncreated Immaculate Conception belongs also to Mary, His Spouse, because She belongs to Him entirely and is wholly united to Him—so much so that, together with Him, She gives existence to the God-Man.

God the Holy Spirit, with the Immaculate, in Her, and of Her, produced His masterpiece: Jesus, God-made-Man. And in this same way—with Her, in Her, of Her—He wants to produce Christ in your soul. The more He will find Mary in your soul, the more He will produce Jesus therein. He will give Himself generously to your soul according to the place you have given to Mary, His Spouse. If He finds Her entirely present in your soul, He will come down into it with great power. He will fill you with His seven gifts and work wonders of grace in you.

Think, too, that one of the main reasons why the Holy Spirit does not work great wonders in souls is that He does not find in them a sufficiently close union with Mary, His inseparable Spouse. He finds few souls who are truly consecrated to Her without limit and reserve.

This is a great mystery of grace which many Christians do not know, even those who are learned and very pious. Now that it has been made known to you, thank the Holy Spirit for it, and seek to be an ever more faithful possession and property of the Immaculate, so that He can come to you and transform you by His power.

Daily Prayers (pp. 85–86)

DAY 28 – ACTION AND REACTION

 ove always comes down from Heaven to earth in the same way: it originates from the Father and is given through the Son and the Holy Spirit to creatures. Any response to that love always returns to God in the same way also: from creation, through the Holy Spirit, through the Son, to the Father. The whole universe is permeated by this Divine law of action and reaction: the Creator's action of love and the creature's reaction to love.

It is the Holy Spirit who initiates the reaction to love. But He never acts alone. The union between the Holy Spirit and Mary His Spouse is so perfect and inexpressibly close that the Holy Spirit acts only through Her and never without Her. Since the very first moment of Her existence, the Giver of Grace, the Holy Spirit, has established His own dwelling place in Her soul. He took such absolute possession of it that the name "Spouse of the Holy Spirit," although true and beautiful, is still nothing but a distant, pale and imperfect shadow of this union.

Do you see, therefore, how the first step of your reaction to Divine Love must always be taken with Mary, without whom the Holy Spirit never acts? Can you now see clearly how the Holy Spirit will not initiate in you the reaction to Divine Love without Her?

If you seek to be docile to the Holy Spirit, be docile to His Immaculate Spouse. He guides souls on their return to God only with Her and through Her, and enkindles in souls a love for Her and confidence in Her. His will is Her will, His action Her action. You can therefore say without scruple and with all confidence use the following expressions: "I want to do the will of the Immaculate"; "Let Her will be done." You must see Her hand in your daily life and, about whatever happens, you can say, "The Immaculate has allowed these things to happen," and you can say this because She never wants anything other than what the Holy Spirit wishes. Her will is in no way different than that of the Holy Spirit, nor of Her Son, nor of the Father. You can let yourself be led by Her without any fear.

Indeed, speaking of Her will without any reservations, you give even greater glory to God, because you confess that you not only love His holy will, but you praise Him and glorify Him for having created a creature so perfect as the Immaculate; a creature so loving as She is, who freely unites Herself to God in everything and who so infallibly unites you to God as well—and for having made Her His own Mother and yours.

Surrender yourself to Her totally—let Her guide you; and be confident that you will reach the very Heart of God Himself.

Daily Prayers (pp. 85–86)

DAY 29 – THE FREEDOM OF A CHILD OF MARY

hen you belong to the Immaculate, all that you can call your own becomes Hers. You become Her possession and property always and in everything you do, and all your actions belong to Her in a special way. God sees you in no other way than as belonging to Her, as a child of Mary.

And although you truly belong to Her, you must remember that She belongs to God, and all that is Hers is God's. For this reason, She with Her whole heart wants you to belong to Him. You must therefore let Her guide you and inspire you to go to God, and to do so without any fear. Know that your consecration to Her does not come at the price of your relationship with God or the saints.

When you pray, it is under Her guidance that you do so—and

because you belong to Her, you can pray directly to the Father, to the Son, to the Holy Spirit, to the angels or to any of the saints. You can do so not only without the least scruple, but with all the greater confidence, because you are always praying with Her and in Her. You are a member of a loving family in which there is no jealousy. When you pray to Our Lord, know for a fact that it is the Immaculate who is inspiring you to pray to Him. When you pray to Her, know that you bring great joy to Our Lord: it is He who inspires you to pray to Her. Be rid of your limited, human way of thinking, so tainted by the experience of human misery and sin, so full of jealousy, rivalry and competition. Let Her guide you in your devotion, always remembering that you are a member of a loving family, the family of God, where there is no strife or competition.

If we are Hers and all that is ours is Hers, then Our Lord will accept everything from us as coming from Her—as Her own possession and property. Whether you can remember this or not, whether you can understand it or not—you will always be seen by Jesus as the special, beloved property of His Mother, and His love for you will be a special love.

And our good Mother will never leave our actions imperfect, but will make them worthy of Herself, that is immaculate, without the slightest blemish. For this reason, you can be sure that even if you do not think of it or remember it or understand it, every prayer made by you to Jesus and every action offered for love of Him will bring an incomparably greater joy to His Most Sacred Heart than if you were not consecrated to His Mother. As long as you do not deliberately exclude Our Lady's mediation or revoke your total, whole-hearted consecration to Her, you can always be at peace; you must never worry about trying to constantly keep the awareness of Her mediation on your mind, because you are incapable of doing this due to your limited human memory and intelligence.

You can let your soul freely follow the inspiration of your heart and all the more confidently approach the Tabernacle, the Cross, the Crib, the Most Holy Trinity and all other holy devotions approved by the Church, because you do not approach on your own, but with Her, as Her child and possession. You can pray freely as the love of God inspires you, and the Holy Spirit—the One who removes all limits to your love—guides you and moves you.

Daily Prayers (pp. 85–86)

DAY 30 – SURRENDER YOURSELF TO HER

O Lord my heart is not lifted up, my eyes are not raised too high;
I do not occupy myself with things too great and too marvelous
for me. But I have calmed and quieted my soul,
like a child quieted at its mother's breast;
like a child that is quieted is my soul.

— PSALM 131

hen you consecrate and surrender yourself to Her, you will experience the same peace the Holy Spirit gave to the Psalmist. Total consecration to the Immaculate is a way of profound humility, and, therefore, of profound peace as well, a great interior peace. Although it is not a path free from pain and tribulation—because it begins on Calvary, at the foot of Our Lord's Cross—it will nevertheless bestow on you a peace in the depth of your soul which cannot be affected by any tribulations that afflict the mere surface.

Rest as a child in your Mother's arms, and let Her lead you through life. Whatever in your life does not depend on your own free will is certainly permitted by Her to happen for your greater good—even if it is something caused by the evil will of others. If She allows it to happen, there is some good in it for you, and She will provide whatever grace you need to face it, to overcome it, to benefit and grow by it—whatever the challenge might be.

See all things in the light of your belonging to the Immaculate. Do not fear life's challenges; respond to them 1) by either not paying attention to them at all, should they be something indifferent, neither helping nor hindering you from drawing closer to Her—such as desolation, misunderstandings and the like; or 2) by using them, accepting them, taking part in them, following them, if they do help you towards this goal of greater union with Her—such as spiritual consolation; or 3) by resisting them and fighting them resolutely and confidently if they hinder this same goal—such as temptations to sin.

In all those things in life where neither necessity nor obedience to legitimate authority has decided a course of action for you, do as you wish, but always try to give the greatest pleasure and consolation to Her Immaculate Heart. Love and do what you wish, as St. Augustine says.

Total consecration to the Immaculate is also a path of great simplicity. It consists in knowing that where She is not present, God is not present there either: neither the Father, nor the Son nor the Holy Spirit. But on the contrary, wherever You find Her, there you find the whole Holy Trinity, there you find supernatural life and the pathway to eternal life.

Your attitude must therefore be one of humility, simplicity and a peaceful and persevering determination to allow yourself to be led by Her always, in all places and in all things. And no matter what might happen around you, you must always come back to Her with everything, and to remain in the peace and love of a child resting in its mother's arms.

Daily Prayers (pp. 85–86)

DAY 31 — FEAR NOTHING

our first consecration to the Immaculate happened on Calvary, not in the midst of consolation, but in pain and sorrow. It was done by the agonizing Jesus and it was received by His sorrowful Mother. Picture in your mind the scene of Calvary: see how She stands there, strong and courageous, at the foot of the cross, without succumbing to the immensity of suffering that engulfs Her. See how She lovingly accepts you as Her child. The Mother of Sorrows Herself, triumphant over suffering, becomes your own Mother! You therefore have nothing to fear from your own sufferings: with Her, you will be able to withstand all of them.

It is certain that satan will seek to attack every soul who wants to approach the Immaculate—and he will lie in wait for Her heel— that is Her children—trying to strike at them, to separate them from Her. She allows this only to more clearly manifest Her power in you. Although satan will try to create storms outside and inside of you to sink you into discouragement and despair; though he will try to make you feel like you cannot endure—if you remain united to Her, all of this will come to no avail—his defeat is sure, your victory certain: the words of Scripture will always be true: She will crush his head (cf. Gen 3:15).

When you become Hers, the Immaculate will not spare you a share in Her own great sufferings. You will receive crosses, but do not be afraid of them. Those who are consecrated to Our Lady carry their crosses with greater ease and gain more merit and glory. What could easily stop another person's progress, or even bring about his downfall, will not stop you at all, but will even help you on your way, because this good Mother will sweeten all the crosses She prepares for you in the honey of Her maternal goodness and the unction of pure love. Though your crosses might be very heavy, when you receive them from Her hands, you will be able to carry them with joy. You must carefully remember that, without Her, you will never be able to carry your crosses, not even the light ones. But with Her you will have the strength to carry all of them, even the heaviest. Without a trusting devotion to the Immaculate, who is the very sweetness of the cross, even the lightest crosses will become unbearable to you, whereas with Her you will not be overwhelmed by even the biggest ones.

Our Lord still speaks to your heart these same words of consecration and beckons you to make the response yourself, on your own, of your own free will: "Behold your Mother!" He says to you. "Do not be afraid of my cross—with Her you will carry it faithfully and you will be victorious over suffering." You will see Our Lady's astounding victories in your life, if you let Her guide you and do not pull back. Fear nothing and stay close to Her. Let Her carry you in Her arms wherever She leads, even in the midst of the fiercest battles. She will always conquer because She is always victorious!

Daily Prayers (pp. 85–86)

DAY 32 – GIVE HER YOUR MERITS

 very grace that comes down to your soul from God the Father comes only through Jesus and the Immaculate. And in no other way can your response to grace return back to the Father, except through Jesus and the Immaculate. Anything that you do under the inspiration of grace—any good work or merit of yours—must pass through Her immaculate hands in order to perfectly return and reach your heavenly Father.

Give Her, therefore, all your good works together with all their merit, which is the heavenly reward that is due to them. Give Her all their satisfactory value, which is their power to make atonement for sin and to obtain graces from God. To safeguard your good works and merits, place no trust in yourself because you know not what to ask (Rm 8:26) and because you carry your treasure in a mere earthen vessel (2Cor 4:7) and you can lose it all in just one moment of weakness. Trust rather in Her power and in Her goodness alone.

By your consecration to Our Lady, you will give to Her all the good that you do, which means the meritorious and satisfactory value of your good works, your penances and your prayers. You will give it to Her that She may keep, increase, and perfect it for you; that She may apply it wherever She pleases and to whomever She pleases, for the salvation of the greatest number of souls and for the greatest possible glory of God. She will receive it from you that She may present it to Jesus for you as Her own, hence immaculate, pleasing to God.

Once you give all this to Her, think of the confidence with which you will be able to pray to Her! You will be able to pray for all your intentions and for all your loved ones knowing that it is not you alone who are praying, but Our Lady with you, whose love is far greater than yours, who cannot make a mistake in asking Jesus or applying graces from Him. She can and will obtain for you more than you could ever obtain on your own, far greater things, beyond what you would even dare to ask. But you must not hold back anything from Her. Do not be afraid to let Our Lady fix your faulty prayers as She sees necessary; to change or improve your petitions if She should see that this is the better thing to do for you; to apply graces to whomever and however She sees fit. Let Her decide everything, without exception.

Banish all worry and anxiety from your heart, as if you had to take care of everything on your own. Our Lady will take special care of all that is yours, because all that is yours will become Hers. If you truly give Her everything—everything and everyone that is dear to your heart—then She will have special concern for all of them. She will never allow Herself to be outdone in goodness and generosity, and will give back to you far more than the little you are able to give to Her.

Most of all, confidently ask Her for the graces She Herself wants to give you, and which you do not know how to even ask for: let Her surprise you and show you Her own loving intentions for you. Our Lady sees what you cannot see—your needs and those of your loved ones—like She saw at the wedding feast in Cana. Trust in Her always and ask Her to give you all that Her motherly Heart wishes.

Daily Prayers (pp. 85–86)

DAY 33 – GIVE HER YOUR EVERYTHING

here are many souls who, in a moment of fervor, have given all to the Immaculate. But there are almost as many who have taken everything back, little by little. In the hour of trial, when their consecration demanded sacrifices, they said, "This is a hard saying, and who can hear it?" And they ceased walking in the way of their total consecration. Will you do as they?

If the mere thought of taking back your consecration frightens you, turn to Our Lady, beg your heavenly Mother incessantly to always keep you in Her Immaculate hands and never let you slip away. Acquire the habit of frequently renewing your consecration to your loving Mother. Renew it at your waking hour so that your whole day may belong to Her. Renew it before your principal actions, in order to recall to mind that it is not for yourself that you ought to act, but solely for Her. Renew it especially in the trials of life. Say to Her then, "O Mother, when I gave myself wholly to you in the enthusiasm of my filial love, I did not foresee this sacrifice. But I did intend to give myself entirely, and I do not want to retract my donation. I accept from You whatever You wish, because You wish it, whatever it may cost me!"

"God loves a cheerful giver" (2Cor 9:7). Rejoice in having given yourself to Her without limits, in being Her child, Her servant, Her property and possession—or whatever other expression the saints have used or will use in the future to express the totality of your consecration to Her. Always remember that total consecration to the Immaculate consists in giving yourself entirely to Her in order to belong entirely to Jesus through Her, in the safest, surest and most beautiful way. This consecration requires you to give to Her: (1) your body with all its senses and members; (2) your soul with all its faculties; (3) your present material possessions and all future ones as well; (4) your interior and spiritual possessions, namely, your merits, virtues and good actions of the past, the present and the future.

In other words, you give Her all you possess, both in your natural life as well as in your supernatural life, together with all that you might acquire in the future in the order of nature, of grace and of glory in Heaven. Nothing must be held back if your consecration is to be total—not even the smallest object or the tiniest good deed. And you must give Her everything for all eternity, wishing as your only reward the honor of belonging to Our Lord through Mary and in Mary.

The Blessed Virgin, on Her part—being the Mother of gentleness and mercy—never allows Herself to be surpassed in love and generosity. When She sees you giving yourself to Her, depriving yourself of what you prize most in order to give it to Her, She will give Herself completely to you, and in a marvelous manner. She will engulf you in the ocean of Her graces, adorn You with Her merits, support you with Her power, enlighten you with Her light, and fill you with Her love. She will share Her virtues with you. She will make up for your failings and become your representative with Jesus. Just as you will belong entirely to Mary, so Mary will belong entirely to you. What St. John says of himself in his gospel, will be likewise true of you: "He took Her for his own."

Daily Prayers (pp. 85–86)

Tomorrow is the day you will make
your consecration to the Immaculate.
In preparation, you can handwrite your act
of consecration and sign it after you have recited it,
but this is not obligatory, and you can simply use
the one provided on p. 73.

Because it is a day special for Our Lady
and for you, if you are able, you should try
to make a good confession, attend Holy Mass
and receive Holy Communion. If possible, recite
your consecration devoutly in church in front of an
image or altar of Our Lady. But even if you cannot
do this and you will make your consecration at
home or some other place, be sure that Our Lady
will be pleased with you nevertheless, as long as
it comes from your heart.

ACT OF TOTAL CONSECRATION TO THE IMMACULATE

by Saint Maximilian M. Kolbe

Immaculate, Queen of heaven and earth, Refuge of sinners and our most loving Mother, God has willed to entrust the entire order of mercy to You. I, an unworthy sinner, cast myself at Your feet, humbly imploring You to take me with all that I am and have, wholly to Yourself as Your possession and property. Please make of me, of all my powers of soul and body, of my whole life, death, and eternity, whatever pleases You. If it pleases You, use all that I am and have without reserve, wholly to accomplish what has been said of You: "She will crush the serpent's head," and "You alone have destroyed all heresies in the whole world." Let me be a fit instrument in Your immaculate and most merciful hands for introducing and increasing Your glory to the maximum in all the many strayed and indifferent souls, and thus help extend as far as possible the blessed Kingdom of the Most Sacred Heart of Jesus. For, wherever You enter, You obtain the grace of conversion and sanctification, since it is through Your hands that all graces come to us from the Most Sacred Heart of Jesus.

℣. Allow me to praise You, O most holy Virgin.

℞. Give me strength against Your enemies.

AFTER YOUR CONSECRATION

Once you have consecrated yourself to the Immaculate, seek to make consecration your way of life. To do so, you can do the following:

✢ Live in close union with Her, praying to Her often and with attention, reverence and devotion.

✢ Recite especially the Hail Mary and the Litany of Loreto; recite the Rosary every day (before saying you are unable, make sure that your being "unable" is not just a being unwilling in disguise!).

✢ Prepare for the feasts of Our Lady with confession and celebrate them by making an effort to receive Holy Communion on these days (for a list of Marian feasts, see the beginning of this booklet, "Choosing a Date" p. 4).

✢ Do everything through, with, in, and for Mary. This means consulting Her before your actions, invoking Her most holy Name frequently, speaking to Her about your feelings and impressions and everything else that happens in and around you.

✢ Associate yourself with Mary in a special way before, during and after Holy Communion.

✢ Every year, commemorate the anniversary of your consecration by a more thorough renewal, following the same 33-day period of meditations or other Marian meditations.

✢ Join the Mission of the Immaculate Mediatrix (MIM), a movement whose members live the spirit of total consecration and dedicate themselves to the Marian apostolate. For more information, see p. 91.

✧ Renew your total consecration every day by reciting the Act of Consecration of St. Maximilian M. Kolbe, or an equivalent act (see shorter act of daily consecration below).

✧ Continue to grow in your knowledge of the Immaculate by reading good books about Her, such as the following:

- *A Treatise on True Devotion to the Blessed Virgin*, by St. Louis de Montfort
- *Life of Union with Mary*, by Fr. Emil Neubert, SM
- *Mary My Mother*, by Fr. Joseph Schryvers, CSsR
- *Who is Mary?*, by Fr. Gabriel M. Pelettieri, FI

SHORTER ACT
OF DAILY CONSECRATION

O Immaculate, Mother of God,
and my Mother, Mary,
I renew my total consecration to You,
and I offer to Your Immaculate Heart
my prayers and works,
joys and sacrifices of this day,
in cooperation with Your mission
of conquering the whole world
for the Kingdom of Christ.

℣. Allow me to praise You, O most holy Virgin.

℟. Give me strength against Your enemies.

PRAYERS FOR EACH WEEK
First Five Days

ACT OF ADORATION
OF THE MOST HOLY TRINITY
by Saint Maximilian

I adore You, our heavenly Father, because
You have deigned to place in the most pure
womb of Mary, Your only begotten Son.

I adore You, O Son of God, because
You condescended to enter the womb of Mary,
and became truly Her actual Son.

I adore You, O Holy Spirit, because
You deigned to form in Her Immaculate womb
the Body of the Son of God.

I adore You, O Most Holy Trinity, O one God
in the Holy Trinity, for having exalted the
Immaculate in such a Divine way.

And I will never cease daily from the first
moment I awake to adore You most humbly,
O Divine Trinity, with my face to the ground,
repeating three times:

Glory be to the Father, and to the Son,
and to the Holy Spirit, as it was in the beginning,
is now and ever shall be, world without end. Amen

Glory be… Glory be…

ACT OF TRUST IN THE IMMACULATE
by Saint Maximilian

Dearest Mother, deign to do with me whatever
is pleasing to You for the greatest glory of God.
I am Yours, my dearest Immaculate Mother. You
see how miserable I am, walking along the edge
of a precipice, full of self-love. If You release
me from Your immaculate hands for even only
one instant, I will be the first to fall into the
most grievous sins and into the bottom of hell.
But if You do not let go of me (although this is
something of which I am completely unworthy)
and will lead me, I will surely not fall and I will
become a Saint, a great Saint.

O Mary conceived without sin,
pray for us who have recourse to You,
and for all who do not have recourse to You,
especially for the enemies of the holy Church,
and those recommended to You.

WEEK 1
Come to the Throne of Grace

ACT OF ADORATION
OF THE MOST HOLY TRINITY
by Saint Maximilian

I adore You, our heavenly Father, because
You have deigned to place in the most pure
womb of Mary, Your only begotten Son.

I adore You, O Son of God, because
You condescended to enter the womb of Mary,
and became truly Her actual Son.

I adore You, O Holy Spirit, because
You deigned to form in Her Immaculate womb
the Body of the Son of God.

I adore You, O Most Holy Trinity, O one God
in the Holy Trinity, for having exalted the
Immaculate in such a Divine way.

And I will never cease daily from the first
moment I awake to adore You most humbly,
O Divine Trinity, with my face to the ground,
repeating three times:

Glory be to the Father, and to the Son,
and to the Holy Spirit, as it was in the beginning,
is now and ever shall be, world without end. Amen

Glory be… Glory be…

SALUTATION OF THE BLESSED VIRGIN
by Saint Francis of Assisi

Hail, O Lady, holy Queen,
holy Mother of God.
You are the Virgin-made-Church, and the one
chosen by the most holy Father in Heaven,
whom He consecrated with His most holy,
beloved Son and with the Holy Spirit,
the Paraclete, with whom there was and is
all the fullness of grace and every good.

Hail, His Palace! Hail, His Tabernacle!
Hail, His Home! Hail, His Robe!
Hail, His Servant! Hail, His Mother!
And hail, all you holy virtues which,
through the grace and light of the Holy Spirit,
are poured into the hearts of the faithful so that,
from their faithless state,
You may make them faithful to God.

O Mary conceived without sin,
pray for us who have recourse to You,
and for all who do not have recourse to You,
especially for the enemies of the holy Church,
and those recommended to You.

(OPTIONAL)

Litany of Loreto, p. 87

WEEK 2

Take Her Into Your Home
(The Spiritual Maternity of Mary)

ACT OF ADORATION
OF THE MOST HOLY TRINITY
by Saint Maximilian

I adore You, our heavenly Father, because
You have deigned to place in the most pure
womb of Mary, Your only begotten Son.

I adore You, O Son of God, because
You condescended to enter the womb of Mary,
and became truly Her actual Son.

I adore You, O Holy Spirit, because
You deigned to form in Her Immaculate womb
the Body of the Son of God.

I adore You, O Most Holy Trinity, O one God
in the Holy Trinity, for having exalted the
Immaculate in such a Divine way.

And I will never cease daily from the first
moment I awake to adore You most humbly,
O Divine Trinity, with my face to the ground,
repeating three times:

*Glory be to the Father, and to the Son,
and to the Holy Spirit, as it was in the beginning,
is now and ever shall be, world without end. Amen*

Glory be… Glory be…

ANTIPHON OF OUR LADY
by Saint Francis of Assisi

Holy Virgin Mary, among women there is
no one like You born into the world.
You are the Daughter and the
Handmaid of the most high and supreme
King and Father of Heaven.
You are the Mother of our most holy
Lord Jesus Christ.
You are the Spouse of the Holy Spirit.
Pray for us, with Saint Michael the Archangel,
and all the powers of Heaven and all the saints,
to Your most holy beloved Son,
our Lord and Master.

O Mary conceived without sin,
pray for us who have recourse to You,
and for all who do not have recourse to You,
especially for the enemies of the holy Church,
and those recommended to You.

(OPTIONAL)

Litany of Loreto, p. 87

WEEK 3
Become Like Your Mother
(Transubstantiation into the Immaculate)

ACT OF ADORATION
OF THE MOST HOLY TRINITY
by Saint Maximilian

I adore You, our heavenly Father, because
You have deigned to place in the most pure
womb of Mary, Your only begotten Son.

I adore You, O Son of God, because
You condescended to enter the womb of Mary,
and became truly Her actual Son.

I adore You, O Holy Spirit, because
You deigned to form in Her Immaculate womb
the Body of the Son of God.

I adore You, O Most Holy Trinity, O one God
in the Holy Trinity, for having exalted the
Immaculate in such a Divine way.

And I will never cease daily from the first
moment I awake to adore You most humbly,
O Divine Trinity, with my face to the ground,
repeating three times:

Glory be to the Father, and to the Son,
and to the Holy Spirit, as it was in the beginning,
is now and ever shall be, world without end. Amen

Glory be… Glory be…

SUPPLICATION TO OUR LADY
by Saint Maximilian

Allow me to praise You, O Most holy Virgin,
with my personal commitment and sacrifice.
Allow me to live, work, suffer, be consumed
and die for You, just for You.
Allow me to bring the whole world to You.
Allow me to contribute to Your ever greater
exaltation, to Your greatest possible exaltation.
Allow me to give You such glory that no one else
has ever given You up to now.
Allow others to surpass me in zeal
for Your exaltation, and me to surpass them,
so that by means of such noble rivalry
Your glory may increase ever more profoundly,
ever more rapidly, ever more intensely
as He who has exalted You so indescribably
above all other beings Himself desires.

In You alone God is incomparably more glorified
than in all His other saints.

For You God has created the world.
For You God has also called me to existence.

Allow me to praise You, O Most Holy Virgin.

O Mary conceived without sin,
pray for us who have recourse to You,
and for all who do not have recourse to You,
especially for the enemies of the holy Church,
and those recommended to You.

(OPTIONAL)

Litany of Loreto, p. 87

WEEK 4
Let Yourself Be Guided by Her

ACT OF ADORATION
OF THE MOST HOLY TRINITY
by Saint Maximilian

I adore You, our heavenly Father, because
You have deigned to place in the most pure
womb of Mary, Your only begotten Son.

I adore You, O Son of God, because
You condescended to enter the womb of Mary,
and became truly Her actual Son.

I adore You, O Holy Spirit, because
You deigned to form in Her Immaculate womb
the Body of the Son of God.

I adore You, O Most Holy Trinity, O one God
in the Holy Trinity, for having exalted the
Immaculate in such a Divine way.

And I will never cease daily from the first
moment I awake to adore You most humbly,
O Divine Trinity, with my face to the ground,
repeating three times:

*Glory be to the Father, and to the Son,
and to the Holy Spirit, as it was in the beginning,
is now and ever shall be, world without end. Amen*

Glory be… Glory be…

RENEWAL OF BAPTISMAL PROMISES

I reject sin, so as to live in the freedom
of God's children.

I reject the glamor of evil and refuse to be
mastered by sin.

I reject satan, father and prince of darkness.

I believe in God, the Father Almighty,
Creator of heaven and earth.

I believe in Jesus Christ, His Only Son,
Our Lord, who was born of the Virgin Mary,
was crucified, died and was buried,
rose from the dead and is now seated
at the right hand of the Father.

I believe in the Holy Spirit,
the Holy Catholic Church,
the communion of saints,
the forgiveness of sins,
the resurrection of the body and life everlasting.
Amen.

*O Mary conceived without sin,
pray for us who have recourse to You,
and for all who do not have recourse to You,
especially for the enemies of the holy Church,
and those recommended to You.*

(Optional)

Litany of Loreto

Lord have mercy.
Christ have mercy.
Lord have mercy.
Christ hear us.
Christ graciously hear us.

God, the Father of heaven, **have mercy on us.**

God the Son, Redeemer of the world, **have mercy on us.**
God the Holy Spirit, **have mercy on us.**
Holy Trinity, one God, **have mercy on us.**

Holy Mary, **pray for us.**
Holy Mother of God, **pray for us.**
Holy Virgin of virgins, **pray ...**
Mother of Christ,
Mother of the Church,
Mother of mercy,
Mother of divine grace,
Mother of hope,
Mother most pure,
Mother most chaste,
Mother inviolate,
Mother undefiled,
Mother most amiable,
Mother most admirable,
Mother of good counsel,
Mother of our Creator,
Mother of our Savior,
Virgin most prudent,
Virgin most venerable,
Virgin most renowned,

Virgin most powerful,
Virgin most merciful,
Virgin most faithful,
Mirror of justice,
Seat of wisdom,
Cause of our joy,
Spiritual vessel,
Vessel of honor,
Singular vessel of devotion,
Mystical rose,
Tower of David,
Tower of ivory,
House of gold,
Ark of the covenant,
Gate of heaven,
Morning star,
Health of the sick,
Refuge of sinners,
Solace of migrants,
Comfort of the afflicted,
Help of Christians,
Queen of Angels,
Queen of Patriarchs,
Queen of Prophets,
Queen of Apostles,
Queen of Martyrs,
Queen of Confessors,
Queen of Virgins,
Queen of all Saints,
Queen conceived without original sin,
Queen assumed into heaven,
Queen of the most holy Rosary,
Queen of families,
Queen of peace.

Lamb of God,
who takes away the sins of the world,
spare us, O Lord.

Lamb of God,
who takes away the sins of the world,
graciously hear us, O Lord.

Lamb of God,
who takes away the sins of the world,
have mercy on us.

Pray for us, O holy Mother of God.
**That we may be made worthy of
the promises of Christ.**

Let us pray.
Grant, we beseech You,
O Lord God,
that we, Your servants,
may enjoy perpetual health of mind and body;
and by the glorious intercession
of the Blessed Mary, ever Virgin,
may be delivered from present sorrow,
and obtain eternal joy.
Through Christ our Lord.
Amen.

CONSECRATE
YOUR LIFE
TO MARY

AS A FRANCISCAN FRIAR OF THE IMMACULATE

🌐 MARYMEDIATRIX.COM

✉ VOCATIONS@MARYMEDIATRIX.COM

MIM
Mission of the Immaculate Mediatrix

A public association of the faithful for laity to live and promote unlimited consecration to Mary, under the guidance of the Franciscans of the Immaculate, and after the example of the great modern apostle and martyr of Auschwitz, Saint Maximilian Mary Kolbe.

JOIN THE MIM!
marymediatrix.com/mim/